Dangerous Sky

Bibliographies of Battles and Leaders

The Central Pacific Campaign, 1943–1944: A Bibliography
James T. Controvich

American Warplanes 1908–1988: A Bibliography
Myron J. Smith, Jr.

Pearl Harbor: A Bibliography
Myron J. Smith, Jr.

The Battles of Coral Sea and Midway, 1942: A Selected Bibliography
Myron J. Smith, Jr.

The Battle of Jutland: A Bibliography
Eugene L. Rasor

The Falklands/Malvinas Campaign: A Bibliography
Eugene L. Rasor

The Normandy Campaign, 1944: A Selected Bibliography
Colin F. Baxter

The Spanish Armada of 1588: Historiography and Annotated Bibliography
Eugene L. Rasor

General Matthew B. Ridgway: An Annotated Bibliography
Paul M. Edwards

The Pusan Perimeter, Korea, 1950: An Annotated Bibliography
Paul M. Edwards

General Douglas MacArthur, 1880–1964: Historiography and Annotated Bibliography
Eugene L. Rasor

The Inchon Landing, Korea, 1950: An Annotated Bibliography
Paul M. Edwards

DANGEROUS SKY

A Resource Guide to the Battle of Britain

Eunice Wilson

Bibliographies of Battles and Leaders,
Number 14

GREENWOOD PRESS
Westport, Connecticut • London

Copyright Acknowledgments

Every reasonable effort has been made to trace the owners of copyright materials in this book, but in some instances this has proven impossible. The author and publisher will be glad to receive information leading to more complete acknowledgments in subsequent printings of the book and in the meantime extend their apologies for any omissions.

Robert Taylor's drawings are reproduced by kind permission of the Military Gallery, Bath, U.K.

Illustrations of badges and decorations are reproduced with permission of the Controller of Her Majesty's Stationery Office.

Library of Congress Cataloging-in-Publication Data

Wilson, Eunice.
Dangerous sky : a resource guide to the Battle of Britain / Eunice Wilson.
p. cm. — (Bibliographies of battles and leaders, ISSN 1056–7410 ; no. 14)
Includes bibliographical references and index.
ISBN 0–313–28216–1 (alk. paper)
1. Britain, Battle of, 1940—Bibliography. I. Title. II. Series.
Z6207.W8W54 1995
[D756.5.B7]
016.94054'211—dc20 94–46943

British Library Cataloguing in Publication Data is available.

Library of Congress Catalog Card Number: 94–46943
ISBN: 0–313–28216–1
ISSN: 1056–7410

First published in 1995

Greenwood Press, 88 Post Road West, Westport, CT 06881
An imprint of Greenwood Publishing Group, Inc.

Printed in the United States of America

The paper used in this book complies with the Permanent Paper Standard issued by the National Information Standards Organization (Z39.48–1984).

10 9 8 7 6 5 4 3 2 1

To those pilots of
247 China British Squadron
who did not come back to
write the history,
and to the survivors and ground staff
without whose help this bibliography
could not have been based on personal experience
as well as
research

One of the most dangerous fashions of our time is the tendency to belittle human beings, to reduce them to the lowest common denominator of greed and self interest or to deny the element of altruism and even heroism in the human character.

—*Dr. Robert Runcie*
Archbishop of Canterbury
RAF Biggin Hill, 21 December 1980

It is not modesty to deny courage, and only those who have never really had to be brave or face danger mock at it. The really brave know they were afraid.

—*Unknown writer*

An example of the short lives of these young men and the courageous but laconic operational records of their squadrons is found in AIR 27/2079–80, the records of 603 City of Edinburgh Squadron, stationed at Hornchurch, Kent, in the path of the attacker.

Pilot Officer P. M. Cardell returned from leave on the 18th December, and was killed in action ten days later.

Another, Flight Sergeant Barwise, 247 Squadron, 1944, arrived on the station, and did not even have time to unpack. Leaving his things, he took off and was missing on his first operation.

—AIR 27/1492–4
Public Record Office, Kew, Surrey

At the end of the Dunkirk evacuation, June 1940, more than one quarter of the pilots of Fighter Command had been killed.

COMMENTS ON FIGHTER COMMAND

19 July 1940—Fighter Command's losses were so great it was clear to the High Command, but fortunately not to the general public, that if things were not altered, within six weeks it would cease to exist.

At Biggin Hill, 32 Squadron slept under their Hurricanes.

At Rochford, 151 slept at readiness in their cockpits and were on call at 3 A.M. for the day's work.

For 609 at Warmwell, there was no running water, the place was dirty and there were no toilets. Conditions were dreadful.

History tells us that the OTUs were never put into action. But training, having been slashed by necessity from six months to two weeks, meant that crews who were still virtually pupils were in action. There was little time for preparation to convert learning into action, although the OTU was meant to be the bridge between theory and fact.

24 August 1940 to 6 September, Fighter Command came near to destruction; pilots were lost simply because they were exhausted. At the week ending 15 September, RAF storage of Spitfires could muster only forty-seven aircraft, and Hurricanes were down to eighty.

The legendary argument over the Big Wing controversy, like the so-called rivalry between

11 and 12 Groups will be discussed in much of the material herewith as is the supposed rivalry between their leaders. The student and researcher must form his/her own opinion and not take hearsay for fact.

Fighter squadrons were moved from place to place to make it look to the enemy as though there were more than there actually were. But some squadrons became so depleted they could not be moved as new green pilots were coming in all the time and needed familiarisation of the area. The World War I story of the *Dawn Patrol* was being repeated, when the leader knew they could not do what was expected of them without experienced pilots. Yet Dowding's Dispatches on the Battle of Britain (see PRO AIR 8/863), written some months after the Battle was over, revealed he had forecast all this when he fought to create Fighter Command, and Churchill had called his pilots the ''chicks'' whom Dowding had defended like a mother hen.

Today, Fighter Command is merged with Bomber Command, into Strike Command, formed 30 April 1968, with headquarters at High Wycombe. Incorporated are Communications, Transport and Coastal Command to make a single multi-role Command.

Contents

Preface

However much you work on RAF research you will never come to the end or know it all. Consider yourself lucky if you come to know well one small but important corner. It is a humbling experience, especially if you are of the same age as these young men of the RAF—many of whom are now only names on a page, on a headstone, or a lost love in someone's heart. If you are younger it will be a different experience, just as moving, just as rewarding. Their average age was twenty. Their commanding officers were older only by a few months. It won't be long now before there are none left to verify the facts contained in the books listed here. But the archival material, the Operational Records, were written while the Battle was being fought over the writers' heads. Whatever fault you find in the records, whatever is omitted that should be there, whatever carelessness in spelling, please remember that it was not retrospect; it was written in the eye of the storm.

These young men are my heroes, many of them unnamed, unknown. These are the young men of whom their elders despaired, in much the same way they think of young frivolity today. These are the young men who, in a few short months, changed the course of the world's history, giving their lives to do so. The triumph of the Battle of Britain was theirs, in spite of being heavily outnumbered. All nationalities were there, not only the British, for Freedom was at stake. In spite of being called the "Brylcream Boys," they came out on top.

Through this research I have come to know them almost personally. Many I met at the time, many since, but the rest were strangers, heroes none the less. We all need heroes, serious authors and first-year students alike, not necessarily as examples. The youngest, smallest, least significant among them, no matter who they were or what they did before the war, had that ability to come through the ordeal even if not now alive to realise it.

Many of the books mentioned will be out of print, although several were reprinted for the fiftieth anniversary year of 1990. They should also be available at the British Library, in second-hand bookshops, or via the public library's lending system. Where imprint and/or date is omitted, it is because they could not be traced via library computer. It is possible such titles were privately printed or are a sponsored industrial print. The titles cover all aspects of RAF research with the Battle of Britain as the focal point. Without its victory there could easily have been no bibliography to assemble.

Acknowledgments

All the publishers who specialise in flying titles and magasines, for sending their lists
Bibliophile
The editors of all magasines mentioned
Fulham and Hammersmith Libraries
Members of the 247 Squadron (F) China British Association
P. J. Moore, posthumously
Kay Priestley
The RAF Museum, Hendon
The Royal Air Force Association (RAFA)
Dr. Robert Runcie
Wg Cdr Robert Stanford-Tuck, posthumously
Eileen Shenton
Eileen Stage
Wg Cdr James Stewart
The staff of the Public Record Office
Sqn Ldr D. W. Warne

Introduction

The Battle of Britain was the most decisive in the European theatre of war, and everyone, civilian and military alike, knew that Britain's freedom depended upon its outcome. France had fallen a few weeks before in that same year of 1940, leaving Britain totally without allies. Thus, if Britain fell, as seemed likely, Europe's fate was sealed.

In 1940, Britain's resources, considerably reduced by the evacuation from Dunkirk, were strained to the utmost. A quarter of the pilots of Fighter Command lost and the bulk of the army left behind in France. Fighter Command, aware that the next stage of the war would be between the Royal Air Force and the Luftwaffe, stepped up the training of pilots, but the time taken to do so was cut to less than half that of peacetime and reduced still further as the war progressed. Aircraft production was increased so that factories worked round the clock shifts. Even so, squadrons often found themselves with insufficient serviceable machines and not enough officers to take command of front line units.

There are no clear parameters with which to define the beginning or the end of the Battle, but mid-July to the end of October 1940 are the accepted dates in which it filled the skies with vapour trails, crashing aircraft, and parachutes falling out of what should have been a beautiful summer.

This was the only battle to be fought over English soil since the Civil War ended at Worcester on 3 September 1651. It is only coincidental that the Second World War began on the same day in 1939, to involve the whole of Britain. The wars of the Scottish Rebellion lasted until the reign of George II but involved only a small area of northern England. No enemy had set foot in England since then, and certainly not by air. The invasion of Wales by the French in

1797 got no further than Pembroke. So the word *England* is chosen deliberately. Though there were sporadic skirmishes in other parts of the United Kingdom, it was over the south coast, and the county of Kent in particular, that most of the fighting took place. Men from all parts of the kingdom took part; auxiliary squadrons of the RAF far from their own home bases were as involved as the rest.

The phrase ''Battle of Britain'' was not coined on the spot but much later; though pilots and ground staff alike knew that this was a crucial turning point, they did not give it a name. The hardest day of all, was when, completely outnumbered, they were confronted with Eagle Day, 13 August. This was the day the Luftwaffe launched a merciless attack on the RAF's airfields. The longest day was 15 September, during which were logged the highest number of claims against the greatest force the Germans had yet sent. So important was that day that it has been ever afterward celebrated as Battle of Britain Day and the week that encloses it as Wings Week, set aside for the support of the RAF Benevolent Fund.

The Luftwaffe's first task was to attack shipping to cut off the remains of the army left in France and so sever its supply lines. Then to follow up with raids and the bombing of airfields still operational prior to the French surrender. Simultaneously, they were to attack airfields on the south coast of Britain to which the RAF fighter squadrons had retreated in order to continue operating. Finally, the attack was to be against towns and cities and to destroy the RAF itself.

It is impossible to draw other than a statistical conclusion from the operations books—ORBs or ops books—of the individual squadrons involved. The daily accounts are laconic and cold, stating the facts without emotion or drama. The end of the month summaries enlarge this only by a little, so that one must read between the lines. Nevertheless, these are the day to day reports from the battle as it was going on, by the pilots themselves to their Intelligence Officers, who had the unenviable task of corroborating claims, proving them correct or otherwise. They also recorded who had not come back and why. The ORBs are therefore the nearest that we who were not there are able to get to the heat of the battle.

It is not easy to search the records of the Royal Air Force in spite of their straightforward documentation. Perhaps because it concerns people we know, love and live with in one context or another. Unlike those of earlier battles, these are our brothers, fathers, uncles, husbands, lovers, grandfathers—they are not yet our ancestors like the others. And there are their friends who survived to confirm it all, as there are not for Agincourt and Waterloo. But if the cold typewritten accounts of their individual battles do not satisfy the hunter after feelings as well as fact, personal experiences written by the survivors will colour the picture, and records of the stations from which they took off fill in the ordinary things that went on in spite of all else.

Take the account of Paul Richey, for example. He was posted as a fighter pilot to No. 1 Squadron at Tangmere, in West Sussex, March 1939. Tangmere was to become the Agincourt of its day, where freedom was hard fought for and won. Paul Richey's graphic account of this famous squadron's activities in France, to where it was posted five days after the declaration of war, goes a long way to explaining the fall of that country and what subsequently led to the Battle of Britain. He was wounded in June 1940 and returned to England medically unfit to fly for the next six months. He saw the Battle from the point of view of a Controller. That gave him the advantage of seeing the scene as whole, though he fretted to get back into line. To see the other side of the same event, comparisons may be made by reading the section on Germany, in particular *The First and the Last,* written by Adolf Galland, one of the Luftwaffe's most distinguished pilots.

It was essential that Hitler, in order to pave the way for an invasion of Britain, should have a strong Luftwaffe which would ensure the RAF's destruction. This would not only leave the country defenceless from the air, its most vulnerable element, but leave the army and navy unsupported and the coastal convoys without protection. The rest would be a walkover. It must have seemed so simple.

Far outnumbering the RAF in aircraft and in pilots, skill and training, the Luftwaffe was able to muster over 2,780 aircraft against Fighter Command's 650 serviceable, ready for action machines and 25 squadrons. Furthermore, Germany's pilots had had considerable experience in Spain, later fully admitted as a "practice run." Except for isolated examples, British pilots had had no such opportunity.

Daily the skies were full of what the press artistically described as the "dance of death." To the men who fought it out they were "dog fights." It is these that are found logged on the Form 540 so familiar to every airman, then as now. The dog fights inevitably resulted in planes shot down and pilots and crews killed, but recruitment was going well. At several stations situations were now arising where there were more men than machines, so much had the imagination of the young been fired. Little more than schoolboys, all aircrew were volunteers, as they still are. Although conscription was in force, no pilot or navigator, nor crew of any bomber, was ever forcibly drafted.

Very little of the highly charged emotions of these few months is reflected in the squadron diaries or in the daily routine orders of their stations. To understand these, the books directly connected by personal experience must be read alongside. To read about the "aces"—a word they hated though it was an official designation indicating more than five certified claims—is to know a little more about Stanford-Tuck, Paddy Finucane, Sailor Malan and Ginger Lacey, to name only a few of the few.

These notes can only be an introduction to the wealth of material available. Each leads on to a potentially wider field of research on which to form an opinion.

Robert Stanford-Tuck in his Hurricane V6864 DT-A, November 1940, from a drawing by Robert Taylor.

There is a sad note to add. Though much of the guidance for this bibliography has come from or is underlined by the experience of those who survived, Wing Commander Bob Stanford-Tuck, DSO, DFC, RAF ret'd, was to have written a foreword to the book. He died before the research was complete.

When the Battle was over and the Luftwaffe retired temporarily defeated, both sides had earned a little respite in which to review their positions. Not unlike in battles of old, the Germans changed their tactics, but still with invasion in mind they now started indiscriminate bombing of the larger cities such as Coventry, Birmingham, Hull and London, especially the latter.

To weaken the morale built up in the civilian population by the RAF's triumph, the German planners must now tackle the offensive from a different angle. Hardly a city in any part of the country escaped the next onslaught. During the twelve weeks that followed, 1,733 enemy aircraft were destroyed as they attempted this massive plan of destruction. In many cases they almost succeeded. But the "Blitz" is another story.

—Air Chief Marshal Sir Denis Smallwood

—Group Captain Peter O'Brian

—Wing Commander Kenneth W. MacKenzie

—Flight Lt James V. Renvoize

Signatures of four Battle of Britain pilots, all of whom were later to serve together in 247 (China British) Squadron. Of these, O'Brian, MacKenzie, and Renvoize fought the Battle in the already outdated Gloster Gladiator biplane. 247 was the only Squadron to do so.

By way of original research at the Public Record Office, in museums dedicated to this period, and the many books which have been written about the Battle, this book's purpose is to bring together as much material as is possible in order to further investigation. Not everything can be included, for there were many more titles published, events occurring, memoires written after it went to press. But the magasines listed can rectify this gap with their reviews and listings. Don't delay in seeking the oral evidence; soon there will be none of the Battle of Britain generation left, time's wingéd chariot being what it is.

Abbreviations

AA	Ack ack, anti-aircraft guns
AAF	Auxiliary Air Force (pre war part-time airmen)
A/C	Aircraft
ADGB	Air Defence of Great Britain
ADJ	Adjutant
ADM	Admiralty Records at Public Records Office (PRO)
AFC	Air Force Cross
AFM	Air Force Medal
AHB	Air Historical Branch, of Ministry of Defence
AMES	Air Ministry Experimental Station
AOC	Air Officer Commanding
ARP	Air Raid Precautions
ATA	Air Transport Auxiliary (Civilian)
ATS	Auxiliary Territorial Service (Women's Section of the Army)
BAFO	British Air Force Overseas
BBC	British Broadcasting Company
BBMF	Battle of Britain Memorial Flight
BC	Bomber Command
BEF	British Expeditionary Force
BL	British Library

BLITZ	Blitzkreig (a short, quick bombardment)
CAS	Chief of Air Staff
CC	Coastal Command
CMG	Companion of the Order of St, Michael and St. George
CO	Commanding Officer
CVO	Commander of the Royal Victorian Order
D DAY	6 June 1944 (D indicated unnamed day)
DFC	Distinguished Flying Cross
DFM	Distinguished Flying Medal
DSO	Distinguished Service Order
FAA	Fleet Air Arm
FC	Fighter Command
FRAES	Fellow of the Royal Aeronautical Society
GAF	German Air Force
Gate Guardian	Postwar example real or replica aircraft. Origin, RAF Regiment.
GCB	Grand Cross of the Bath (a knight)
GCM	Good Conduct Medal
GCVO	Grand Cross of the Royal Victorian Order
GLRO	Greater London Record Office
GP	Group
GRO	General Registrar's Office
HDU	Home Defence Unit
HM	His or Her Majesty
HMSO	His (Her) Majesty's Stationery Office (Government Publications)
HO	Home Office
HQ	Headquarters
JU	Junkers, German Bomber
K IN A	Killed in Action
K ON A S	Killed on Active Service (not against the enemy)
LBC	London Broadcasting Company, local radio
LDV	Local Defence Volunteer (Home Guard)
LG	London Gazette
LOGS	The personal record book kept by aircrew
MI	Military Intelligence
MI5	Security within UK
MAF	Ministry of Agriculture and Fisheries (food)

MAP	Ministry of Aircraft Production
MBE	Member of the Order of the British Empire
MC	Military Cross
ME	Messerschmitt
MoD	Ministry of Defence (the three services are now amalgamated)
MS, MSS	Manuscript, manuscripts
MSFU	Merchant Service Fighter Unit
MU	Maintenance Unit
OBE	Officer of the Order of the British Empire
OC	Officer Commanding (not same as CO, Commanding Officer)
OPERATIONAL	On Operations Against the Enemy
ORB	Operational Record Book
OTU	Operational Training Unit
PAF	Polish Air Force
PLC	Public Limited Company
PM	Prime Minister
PMC	Personnel Management Centre
POW	Prisoner of War
PRO	Public Record Office (Ruskin Avenue, Kew, Surrey, UK)
PRU	Photographic Reconnaissance Unit
RAAF	Royal Australian Air Force
RADAR	Radar Detection and Ranging. Location by radio
RAF	Royal Air Force
RCAF	Royal Canadian Air Force
RFC	Royal Flying Corps. Became RAF in 1918
RN	Royal Navy
RNAF	Royal Netherlands Air Force
RNAS	Royal Naval Air Service
RNOAF	Royal Norwegian Air Force
RNZAF	Royal New Zealand Air Force
SIS	Secret Intelligence Service (external to UK)
SOE	Special Operations Executive (undercover operations)
SQN	Squadron
SSQ	Station Sick Quarters
2 TAF	Second Tactical Air Force
TV	Television

UFO	Unidentified Flying Object
UK	United Kingdom (Great Britain—England, Scotland, Wales and N. Ireland)
ULTRA	Decoding and cypher equipment
USAAF	United States Army Air Force, Army Air Corps or USAF
VC	Victoria Cross (Britain's highest award)
VR	Volunteer Reserve
WAAF	Women's Auxiliary Air Force (later WRAF—Women's Royal Air Force) Both sexes are now all RAF.
WO	War Office
WRNS	Women's Royal Naval Service
WW1	World War 1
WW2	World War 2
Y	Secret Decoding Services, RAF's Intercept System

RAF RANKS SHOULD BE ADDRESSED AS FOLLOWS:

CAS	Chief of Air Staff (or in full)
ACM	Air Chief Marshal (or in full)
AVM	Air Vice Marshal (or in full)
Air Cdr	Air Commodore
Gp Capt	Group Captain
Wg Cdr	Wing Commander
Sqn Ldr	Squadron Leader
Flt Lt	Flight Lieutenant
Fg Off	Flying Officer
Plt Off	Pilot Officer
W/O	Warrant Officer
Flt Sgt	Flight Sergeant
Sgt	Sergeant
Cpl	Corporal
LAC	Leading Aircraftman
LACW	Leading Aircraftwoman
AC_1	Aircraftman 1st class
ACW_1	Aircraftwoman 1st class
AC_2	Aircraftman 2nd Class
ACW_2	Aircraftwoman 2nd class

These ranks do not necessarily indicate only flying (air) crew but can also mean ground and administrative staff. They are ranks, not job descriptions, though GD after the rank of officers indicates air crew. Please refer to the Air Force List (a government publication) for further information.

COMMON TERMS

Adler Tag	Eagle Day, 13 August 1940, the start of the German air offensive against Great Britain.
Gate Guardian	Originally the soldiers of the RAF. Post war the term is used for genuine or replica aircraft of the types that had flown from a station that no longer needed soldiers to guard it.
Logs	Personal record books kept by the air crew.
Luftflotte	A Group in the Luftwaffe.
Operational	Ready for operations against the enemy.
Overlord	Code word for D-Day landings on Normandy, 6 June 1944.
Sea Lion *(Seelowe)*	Codeword for the proposed day of the German invasion of Britain, to follow Adler Tag.
Stalag Luft	Air Force prison camp in Germany.
Station	The airfield or place where an RAF unit is quartered. Also now called a base.

1

General Guidelines for RAF Research

RAF RESEARCH

ALL RESEARCH SHOULD BEGIN WITH WHAT IS KNOWN and work toward that which is not known. In RAF terms, the former generally is the station on which squadrons were located. If not the place, the number of the squadrons. Since squadrons were moved about in order to rest them or to create an appearance which made the enemy believe there were more in the front line than in fact, many squadrons were brought in from other areas when it was clear the Battle of Britain was imminent. Later, squadrons were moved away when combat fatigue began to show, so the place at which a squadron was stationed was therefore not permanent. Its number, however, was, unless and until renumbered or amalgamated with another squadron.

The best books for the initial location study are in a series called Action Stations, which describes in full historical detail each area of the United Kingdom involved. These titles are also separately listed under authors, but hereby listed by county or area. Not all were directly involved in the Battle, but include those on front line battle stations and others involved by training, reinforcements and replacements of aircraft and crews. Although the Action Station series covers the whole country, it was primarily squadrons in the south and south east that were directly involved, although many originated from these other areas. The series is published by Patrick Stephens and Thorsons. Wellingborough, Northamptonshire.

1. *The Military Airfields of East Anglia*, Michael J. F. Bowyer.
2. *The Military Airfields of Lincolnshire and the East Midlands*, Bruce Barrymore Halpenny.

3. *The Military Airfields of Wales and the North West*, David Smith.
4. *The Military Airfields of Yorkshire*, Bruce Barrymore Halpenny.
5. *The Military Airfields of the South West*, Chris Ashworth.
6. *The Military Airfields of the Cotswolds and Central Midlands*, Michael J. F. Bowyer.
7. *The Military Airfields of Scotland, the North East and Northern Ireland*, David J. Smith.
8. *The Military Airfields of Greater London*, Bruce Barrymore Halpenny.
9. *The Military Airfields of the Central South and South East*, Chris Ashworth.
10. *The Military Airfields Supplement and Index*, edited by Bruce Quarrie.

Greater London refers to the area immediately surrounding the capital. The Greater London Record Office (GLRO), where historical documents related to the area may be found, is located on Northampton Rd., London EC1. Do not confuse this with the GRO, the Office of the General Registrar, where indexes of births, marriages and deaths are located. The GRO is at St. Catherine's House, Kingsway, London WC2. Certificates relating to people involved in the Battle of Britain may be obtained there.

To place squadrons on their correct stations, use the following works in conjunction with the above (all three are on the open shelves at the Public Record Office at Kew):

Halley, James, *Squadrons of the RAF* (Tonbridge, Kent: Air Britain, 1988).

Moyes, Philip J. R., *Bomber Squadrons of the RAF* (London: Macdonald and Jane's, 1976).

Rawlings, John D., *Fighter Squadrons of the RAF* (London: Macdonald and Jane's, 1976).

See also these privately published works:

Willis, Steve, and Barry Hollis, *Military Airfields in the British Isles*. The omnibus edition is available direct from the authors at Titchmarsh, Kettering, Northants NN9 5SE. It is also on the PRO's open shelves. Contains 653 wartime sites of the RAF, RN, Allied and US Army Air Forces, described by maps, groups, order of battle and specification.

Jefford, Wg Cdr C. G., MBE, *RAF Squadrons* (Shrewsbury: Airlife, 1988). Records, movements and equipment of all RAF squadrons and their antecedents since 1912. Comprehensive, detailed and essential.

PRELUDE TO THE BATTLE: DUNKIRK

There was barely any breathing time between the Fall of France and the start of the Battle of Britain for the RAF to recoup and reorganise. These accounts of the first months of 1940, before the Battle begins, are essential reading. See A. J. Barker, Richard Collier, Raymond Collishaw, A. E. Clouston, David Divine, Sir Victor Goddard and F. Majdalany.

DETAILED OVERVIEW OF THE BATTLE OF BRITAIN

The Dowding Despatches can be found in AIR 8/863 at the PRO. This is the personal and first hand account of the Battle of Britain by the architect of Fighter Command and the master mind of the RAF's major battle, Air Chief Marshal Sir Hugh C.T. Dowding, GCB GCVO CMG ADC. The copyright is held by his son, the 2nd baron, and it must not be reproduced without his and the PRO's permission. It was very secret, marked in red "to be kept under lock and key."

The Air Council and the Air Board produced 107 volumes yearly from 1916 to 1954. These can be found at the PRO under AIR 6. The Battle of Britain year is particularly interesting.

"A Chronology of the Second World War" was produced by the Royal Institute of International Affairs, Chatham House, London. The 1947 volume was compiled by Mrs N. Hall.

2

The RAF in 1940

SQUADRONS AVAILABLE ON 7 JULY 1940

Throughout the RAF documents at the PRO, a record of the order of battle for the days and the squadrons available will be found intermittently. An example of this follows.

As of 7 July 1940 the RAF had available 52 squadrons in three Groups (10 Group forming since January became operational later in the month); of these, 19 Squadrons had Spitfires, 25 had Hurricanes, 2 had Defiants and 6 had Blenheims. Out of 800 aircraft, 644 were available for operations; of 1,456 pilots, 1,259 were nominally present for duty (197 short of establishment). These were Dowding's "chicks"—the Battle of Britain pilots.

A Fighter squadron generally consisted of 12 aircraft, grouped into four sections of three each, two day, two night, each comprising a Flight, each led by a Flight Commander. When and where possible, in theory, an equal number of aircraft and pilots was held in reserve—two pilots to each operational aircraft, one off, one on. This was not always possible of course, and in the early years several squadrons could not always be kept up to strength.

Two or more squadrons often shared the same airfield, with several airfields under a Sector station which was their HQ. In turn, Sectors made up a Group of which II Group was dominant in the Battle of Britain, with 12 to the north and 10 to the west sharing the responsibility. Each squadron had its own support and ground maintenance staff. A different system, similar to that used by the Luftwaffe, was adopted after the Battle of Britain. Before joining 2 TAF and taking part in D-Day, numbered and moveable "airfields" became the pattern.

These were not fields as such, but groups of two or more squadrons maintained by the same Service Echelon instead of by their own ground staff. This does not apply to the Battle of Britain stations, however.

A Group consisted of several squadrons in Sectors. Neither the number of squadrons nor Sectors was uniform; it depended and still depends upon the need for defence of a particular area. Thus in the Battle of Britain, the southern Groups had more Sectors, and each Sector had more squadrons, than those in the far north, being more vulnerable. The southeast Group, No. 11, had the largest number of Groups/Sectors. The number of squadrons in each Sector and Group was similarly variable. Each Group had a number: 11 Group was for the immediate defence of London; 10 on its western side and 12 on its northern were its support and were frequently drawn in for assistance as well as their own local responsibilities.

The history of Fighter Command is told in the works: Chaz Bowyer, *Fighter Command 1936–68* (London: J. M. Dent, 1980), and Peter Wykeham, *Fighter Command* (London: Putnam, 1960). Both contain good Battle of Britain detail, squadron dispositions by Group for that year, and have excellent bibliographies.

THE STAGES OF THE BATTLE

To help the reader fit the titles of the bibliography into the correct sequence, it is necessary to understand the sequence of the battle itself.

First phase, 10 July–7 August: the contact phase. France surrenders. Fighter sweeps over France.

Second phase, 8 August–23 August: the struggle for command of the air; dog fights over south and southeast England, ground attacks and attacks on the aircraft industry.

Third phase, 24 August–6 September: attack on Britain's factories.

Fourth phase, 7–30 September: Day and night bombing on London and area.

Fifth phase, 1–31 October: Daylight fighter bomber attacks, mainly on London (normally acknowledged as the end of the Battle and the start of the Blitz).

Sixth phase, 14 November: start of the German campaign against Russia.

Outstanding dates to remember include:

5 August 1940: *Adlerangriff*, Attack of the Eagles (German).

10 August: *Adler Tag* (Eagle Day), adverse weather caused the date to be changed to the 13th.

15 August: Luftflotte 2, 3, and 5 engaged; The Big Battle.

17 August: Spitfire/Hurricane losses exceeded those in storage for the first time. CROs (civilian repair organisations) were brought into use.

20 August: "Never in the field of human conflict was so much owed by so many to so few"—Churchill's famous speech, never to be forgotten.

See Richard Collier's *Eagle Day*, which contains a very good bibliography of published and unpublished sources (Hodder and Stoughton, 1966; London: J. M. Dent, 1980, illustrated edition).

A book which sets the scene into date order is the *Chronology of the Second World War*, produced by The Royal Institute of International Affairs, a non-political and unofficial body which encourages the study of international affairs and is prohibited by its Royal Charter from expressing an opinion. There are 29 pages covering 1940; dates given are unbiased and merely a statement of fact. Other useful sources are the *Times Index*, which can be cross referenced with the newspaper for detailed assessment; and the *Annual Register* (copies at the PRO and larger libraries).

THE MAIN EVENTS OF 1940

A chronology of the major events leading up to and including the Battle of Britain follows.

1939

1 September	Germany invades Poland.
2 September	Britain and France, in support of Poland, deliver ultimatum to Germany. Accelerated preparations for the British Expeditionary Force (BEF) to move to France; the force includes the bulk of the British army then mobilised, plus several squadrons of RAF fighters and bombers.
3 September	Britain declares war on Germany, no answer to the ultimatum having been received. The air raid sirens sound almost immediately, a false alarm.
5 October	Polish military resistance finally crushed by German army.
17 December	Empire Air Training Scheme signed in Ottawa. First Canadian troops arrive in Britain.

October 1939 to April 1940—the period of the "phoney war"; very little actual combat. Propaganda leaflets dropped on Germany.

1940

8 January	Food rationing begins.
9 April	Germany invades Norway and Denmark.
10 May	Germany invades Belgium, the Netherlands, Luxemburg. All capitulate. British fighter squadrons reinforced in France.
11–12 May	Munchen-Gladbach raid by British bombers. Two VCs awarded, to F/O D. E. Garland and posthumously to Sgt T. Gray.
13 May	German break through French defences, start of offensive planned to trap Allied armies. Maginot Line gives way. Churchill's "blood, and sweat and tears" speech.

15 May	Dutch army capitulates.
16 May	British Government warned by Air Chief Marshal Sir Hugh Dowding that to send more fighters to France will leave Britain almost defenceless, and that the Allied situation there seems increasingly hopeless.
19 May	After much debate Churchill agrees no additional fighter squadrons will go to France. Some operated from southern UK bases; most did not have sufficiently long range to prolong action over France. BEF begins withdrawal.
20 May	German forces reach Channel coast of France, trapping the BEF inland. Most soldiers have to make their own way back as best they can.
23 May	BEF on half rations.
26 May–4 June	Evacuation of the greater part of the BEF from the Dunkirk beaches by the navy and small civilian boats from England, includes many Allied servicemen now without a country. Many taken prisoner, would-be rescuers among them. RAF accused by army of not being there for protection. It was not realized they were fighting a rearguard action with short-range engines, keeping the Luftwaffe away from the vulnerable beaches. Many valuable aircraft with well-trained, experienced pilots and ground crews left behind.
28 May	Defeat turned into a kind of victory by the courage of the "little ships" over this period until 2/3 June. 225,585 British and 112,546 French and Belgian troops evacuated.
31 May	Roosevelt's Million Dollar Defence Plan.
4 June	Germans claim Dunkirk, taking 40,000 prisoners.
4 June	Churchill's speech—"We shall fight on the beaches, we shall fight in the fields. . . . we shall never surrender."
5 June	The Battle of France.
8 June	The *Carinthia* and HM Aircraft Carrier *Glorious* sunk, the latter with even more loss to the already depleted RAF.
10 June	Italy declares war on Britain and France.
14 June	Germans enter Paris.
17 June	Humiliating defeat forces France to ask for an armistice and "peace" terms, leaving Britain totally alone. All three services seriously understrength.
22 June	Reluctant armistice. (French)
9 July	Another peace offer made by Hitler. Refused.
10 July	The Battle of Britain begins its first phase, which lasts until August, during which the Luftwaffe attack British convoys in the Channel bringing vital supplies. South coast ports also attacked in order to tempt the RAF into action against large formations of German aircraft now based much nearer and within range on newly acquired French airfields.

16 July — Hitler orders German preparations to be made for invasion of Britain at strategic places along the south coast. RAF squadrons brought down from the north for defence of naval concentrations and dockyards in the west.

17 July — Rain. More and more Luftwaffe units brought into action even in bad visibility. 64 Squadron attacked off Beachy Head. German night fighters test out their radio guidance beams over Britain. UK night fighter training increased.

18 July — 610 Squadron from Biggin Hill attacked by Bf 109s, which escape without loss. Suggested they knew how British radar worked. Only one of several similar daily attacks on other stations in this and the following weeks.

19 July — Hitler issues another "plea for peace" to the British, which means only their surrender. The pattern as before. RAF losses so high it is feared Fighter Command will cease to exist in under six weeks. Hitler's Adlerangriff (Attack of the Eagles—the air attack preceding the planned German invasion of Britain) and Adlertag (Eagle Day—the start of the air attack [Battle of Britain]) had not yet started; both postponed, once for weather but mainly without known reason. RAF claims exaggerated in order to keep up civilian morale. Boulton Paul aircraft sent into battle. Not successful.

22 July — Britain rejects Hitler's peace offer. "Who does he think we are?"

24 July — The names Adolf Galland and Werner Molders, Germany's well-known Ace fighter pilots, occur again and again in RAF records, as British fighter pilots meet them in combat. Many airfields flooded by bad weather; conditions difficult.

25 July — A fine day. Convoy in Channel attacked by Bf 100s, attacked in turn by Hurricanes of 32 Squadron, Biggin Hill, 615 Squadron from Kenley, and Spitfires of 54 Squadron. Joe Kennedy, U.S. Ambassador, father of the future President, had little faith in Britain's survival. British Foreign Office records say he told neutral journalists that Hitler would be in London by 15 August. He didn't know the British.

28 July — Another fine day. "Sailor" Malan, a South African in the RAF, meets the Luftwaffe's ace Werner Molders, who has 26 victories to his credit already, not for the first time. With difficulty Molders gets his Messerschmitt back to base and himself, with wounded legs, into hospital. Until now, German rescue planes painted with white crosses have been respected, even if near to Allied shipping. Now suspect, they are warned they will be shot down. Some RAF pilots unwilling to comply with this order. Command is proved right.

1 August	Directive from Hitler to the Luftwaffe: the German Air Force is to overcome and destroy the British air force with all the means at its disposal and as soon as possible. The new offensive is to be called Adlerangriff, the Attack of the Eagles. Adlertag is to be between 9 and 13 August. German leaflet attack on southern England begins on 1–2 August.
3 August	Hitler in Berlin to launch Eagle Day, but bad weather puts it back from the agreed date. Plans for German sea offensive set for 15 September. Raids in southwest 415 sorties flown by Fighter Command, at no cost. Minelayers work during the night. Bombers attack Orkneys and Firth of Forth, intending a pincer movement. Observer Corps in Gravesend put out of action; cornfields in Essex set alight. Visibility 2–5 miles.
4 August	Reconnaissance all day over south coast. Slight respite for Fighter Command on a cloudy day. 261 sorties, no score either side.
5 August	Adlerangriff—Attack of the Eagles—postponed again. Unknown to the British, invasion temporarily called off. Shipping attacked. 65 Squadron destroys a German intruder at 8 A.M. High temperatures. 41 and 151 Squadron attacks 30 to 40 German aircraft. 402 sorties flown.
6 August	Only seven hostile planes reach English coast. Score at the end of the day: one all. Home Defence Units (HDUs) fully occupied on east and southeast coast intercepting German radar and relaying to local RAF Command as well as HQ Fighter Command at Stanmore. See F. H. Hinsley, *British Intelligence in Second World War* (London: HMBO, 1981, 3 vols.), vol. 1.
7 August	German operations light because aircraft largely involved on convoy duties in preparation for Adlerangriff. Fighters fly 393 sorties. General Sander broadcasts to the German people, saying that the main weapon will be the bomber.
8 August	18 Ships and 4 RN destroyers had been lost this day. Coal colliers had to sail in convoy to arrive in Dover from north before dark. Convoy CW9, code name, "Pewitt," lost 16 ships; only 4 out of 20 got through to Dorset. Fighter Command, specifically designed for the protection of the southern coastline, had no adequate air sea rescue. 18 motorboats tried to provide coverage. Few men could remain conscious for more than two hours in the sea.
10 August	German preparations for invasion speed up. Adverse weather causes delay of Adlertag (Eagle Day).
11 August	W/O Edward Mayne, flying with Malan in 74 (Tiger) Squadron, making a tight turn, blacks out and falls in his

Spitfire 4 miles down the sky, about 20,000 feet, before recovery. He is over 40, well over the age limit, and probably the only RFC veteran to fly a Spitfire in the Battle of Britain.

13 August

Unknown to those who woke early this day and to many pilots themselves, this was Eagle Day. The Germans thought the RAF had only limited radar control and that they would be met only by local fighters, being under the impression they had put the radar stations out of action the day before. The jargon had not been understood. They got the weather forecast wrong. A heavy day nonetheless. The second phase begins—main Luftwaffe targets were now the airfields on the south and west coasts as well as radar installations, naval establishments, and aircraft factories all over the country. Object: to destroy the RAF's supports. Losses in Britain are high and worrying; though fighter squadrons maintain a one to one ratio, deeply trained prewar pilots being lost; pilot training and recruitment stepped up, time allowed cut short. But all aircrew are still volunteers; there was no compulsion throughout the war.

The Scandinavian Campaign brings more great losses—the aircraft carrier HMS *Glorious*, bringing back the squadrons of Gladiators which had fought there, is sunk, and all but one of the Blenheims over the Altborg airfield fails to return.

14 August

Little activity during the night; cloudy over the Channel, also the following day. Luftwaffe targets are mainly the southeast and southwestern airfields. Communications Units and installations of all kinds are attacked. Though enemy sorties are only a third of the day before, 91 bombers and 398 bombers took part. 609 Squadron, though inland at Middle Wallop, raided, as is 30 MU (Maintenance Unit) at Sealand, Cheshire. For names of those who took part on both sides see *Strike from the Sky* by Alexander McKee (Souvenir Press, 1960), which has a good map of UK and German Fighter Commands.

15 August

All three fighter wings of the Luftwaffe made heavy raids in clear weather. This was to be the most concentrated of the Campaign. The object was to wreck airfields and radar and to bring as much of the RAF into the air as possible. Intention: total destruction. From Norway to Brittany Britain was the focus. They partly succeeded since the key Chain Home stations of Rye and Dover were put out of action. 54 and 501 squadrons met the attack. Before long every front line squadron was engaged and reserves alerted. A full and detailed description is in *The Narrow Margin* by Derek Wood and Derek Dempster.

16 August — Airfields of Kent, West Sussex and Hampshire severely attacked. Others in Oxfordshire, Suffolk and Essex suffered widespread damage. Radar stations out of action. Goering jubilant. During the night many smaller attacks. A sunny summer's day, even so. Luftwaffe HQ stated that 372 Spitfires, 179 Hurricanes and 21 others had been destroyed. This was the day the famous airfield of Tangmere was almost obliterated and, among many others, the American pilot Billy Fiske was killed. He was the first U.S. citizen to die in the Battle and is buried at Boxgrove, nearby. Full details and pictures in Winston G. Ramsey, ed, *The Battle of Britain, Then and Now*. Diversionary attacks north of the Humber intentionally drew off some of the defensive fighters.

17 August — For the first time Spitfire/Hurricane losses exceeded those in storage. RAF now faced acute pilot shortage, and flights were limited to reconnaissance. Some attacks were made in the Midlands, South Wales and on Merseyside. All Groups drawn into the battle. CROs (civilian repair organisations) brought into use.

18 August — Airfields in the southeast and east attacked by massed Luftwaffe formations again. Bristol, East Anglia and South Wales bombed. This cloudy Sunday was the last all-out effort of the Luftwaffe. Croydon in south London withstood 19 bombs on the airfield; 27 aircraft were destroyed and 10 pilots killed. JU 87s were pulled out of the fight as their losses were too high.

19 August — Isolated raids now on Britain; reconnaissance the main activity. The pace was slowing down. Harassing raids kept the RAF busy, but the slacking of interest enabled them to stand off and recoup, bringing fresh young pilots to the front who had thought it was all going to be over before they could get in.

20 August — A cloudy day with rain moving down from the north. Scattered raids in the morning; southeast airfields attacked in afternoon by waves of aircraft coming in from Calais to attack the balloon barrage. Convoys attacked. Polish Air Force had its first real success over Britain—302 Squadron destroyed a Junkers 88. Churchill's "Never in the field of human conflict... was so much owed by so many to so few" speech.

21 August — Airfields attacked again during the day, Scotland at night. Bad weather reduced the Luftwaffe to tip-and-run raids.

22 August — Industrial attacks in the Midlands at night. During the day shipping reconnaissance and attacks on convoys. So many RAF crews lost through drowning that Air Sea Rescue

services were increased by combining RAF launches and naval auxiliary patrols under local naval authorities.

23 August — Main target South Wales; single raids in the south. Low clouds and rain. Outer London, St Albans, Tangmere, Portsmouth, Abingdon, Biggin Hill, Colchester, Harwich, Cromer, Southampton, Maidstone and others were attacked. Dunlop Rubber's Birmingham Works were attacked with other sources of vital supplies.

24 August — With this Saturday began the third and last stage of the Battle. Heavy attacks of Portsmouth and the naval dockyards. Fighter Squadrons such as 247 brought from the north to reinforce the area. RAF Manston evacuated; big attacks on southeast airfields. Cloudless day when 100 aircraft attacked Dover, North Weald, Hornchurch, Duxford, and Ramsgate; all responded. Fires burning in London heralded the shape of the future. August 24/25 heavy and widespread night bombing by GAF. More raids in southwest; at night the main attack was in the Midlands but spread as far as the north of Scotland. But now 81 British bombers were heading for Berlin. The first of several reprisal raids offered a breathing space for Fighter Command.

26 August — Widespread Luftwaffe raids on industrial targets. Kent and Essex airfields attacked to prevent bomber defence. Nos. 10 and 11 Groups heavily engaged over Portsmouth and Warmwell. 787 sorties flown by Fighter Command, but four pilots lost near Portsmouth and 12 wounded.

27 August — Reconnaissance in the naval dockyard area of Portsmouth and Southampton. Southeast heavily raided. Controversy about big wing flights versus squadron formation flying. Rivalry of 11 and 12 Groups continued, which cost Keith Park his command of 11 Group. Bombs dropped near Bentley Priory, Fighter Command HQ. More and more Allied pilots coming to join RAF after escaping from occupied countries. National squadrons being formed.

28 August — More airfield attacks. First major attack on Liverpool consisted of 100 fighters escorting two groups of Dorniers. A German Gotha trainer with mail for the forces came down on Lewes racecourse almost intact. Intelligence Officers took advantage. System of air raid warnings were Yellow: Fighter Command to areas in path of raiders; Purple: at night similarly, all exposed lighting in docks must be extinguished; Red: the public warned when sirens were sounded. All the information to be passed on, obtained from the Observer Corps.

29 August	More airfield attacks in southeast. Main target, Liverpool. Single raids over wide area. Fair, bright days. Shipping raids. Sixteen squadrons intercepted. Radar stations out of action. Three waves of attack. Detling airfield hit by 50 bombs, totally out of action. Thirty-nine killed, 26 injured at Biggin Hill. More bombers to Midlands, South Wales and London. On the night of August 30/31 raiders came in from 8:30 A.M. onwards in a continuous stream.
31 August	Fighter Command's heaviest losses when southern and eastern airfields were the main target. This Saturday 39 aircraft were shot down with 14 of their pilots killed. In the same 24 hours the Luftwaffe lost 41 aircraft. Raids began at 8 A.M. followed by three waves.
1 September	Growing fatigue was now resulting in increased losses among pilots. Biggin Hill, which had suffered six raids in three days, had its operations room reduced to rubble. Many were killed; two WAAF telephone operators received the Military Medal for staying at their posts (for pictures see Winston G. Ramsey, ed., *The Battle of Britain, Then and Now*). The remaining daylight raids on airfields and the docks at Tilbury opened the next phase on 7 September. In a final attempt to break morale, attacks on London at night.
2 September	Airfields again attacked in four main phases. Widespread raids over Midlands, Liverpool and Wales. Luftwaffe still determined to undermine morale and eliminate squadron defence. They were obviously still intent on preparations for the invasion of Britain. Thirty aircraft wrecked on the ground at Detling.
3 September	Anniversary of the outbreak of war was celebrated by heavy Luftwaffe raids on airfields, but with equal losses. Liverpool and South Wales once more targets in fine weather. Formations built up over Calais from 8 A.M., but only one reached its target intact. Czech pilots of 310 Squadron at Duxford played an important part. (This airfield now houses the air branch of the Imperial War Museum). Once again losses were equal. Damage at Chester and Sealand as bombers reached Liverpool.
4 September	More airfield attacks as well as on such main supply factories as Vickers at Brooklands, Surrey, making Wellington bombers. More night raids on Liverpool. Luftwaffe had been given orders to destroy at least 30 British aircraft factories and those factories producing engines and propellers, together with their ancillary suppliers. At Vickers 88 people were killed and 600 injured. Fighter Command lost 17 aircraft to the Luftwaffe's 25. Everybody was involved now. Over 200 bombers were over

	England that night, at Newcastle, Halifax, Manchester, Nottingham. Tilbury and Gravesend were hit.
5 September	Special cover ordered for fighter factories while great and continuous activity over the whole of Britain lasted. It was a re-creation of the film *Fire over England*, the story of the Tudor reign of Queen Elizabeth I. Enemy bombers began to fly higher to avoid fighter attacks from 10 Group, which was now mainly occupied in fighter factory cover. Higher flying Spitfires being developed.
6 September	Three main attacks but less activity on the whole, largely harassings. Fine weather but cooler. Attempt on Hurricane production at Hawkers; half the total production was made here. Fighters on patrol warded off serious damage.

This marks the official ending of the Battle as the attacks waned and the Luftwaffe withdrew. But no battle has a precise beginning or end, and the effects, at least, were to continue. The high-level bombing of London—the Blitz—was about to begin. After a brief pause, this was to be the final effort before the proposed Invasion of Britain.

13 September	The ship *City of Benares* sailed from Liverpool with 408 passengers on board. It was sunk by U Boat 48 on 17 September. Of 90 children on board being evacuated from the war zone, only 13 were saved. No more were evacuated abroad after this; most were sent out of the cities into the country, especially away from the southeast of England. The book *Children of the Benares* tells their stories through the survivors.

In AIR 16/619 at the PRO is the correspondence concerning the supposed offer to defect of Hitler's personal pilot, Hans Baur, in February 1941. Was this a result of the Luftwaffe's defeat in 1940 or an elaborate plot to fool the RAF's High Command and with them the rest of Britain? Hitler, of course, would know nothing about the plan if such it was, and only the Station Commander at Lympne, Sqn Ldr D. H. Montgomery, was informed by the Chief of Fighter Command. Details of the landing and defection were arranged, but Baur never came. Was it a hoax, or was he discovered, relieved of his command and suitably dealt with? It would seem not, for he lived to write a book. Check this against the station records of Lympne in AIR 28/509 for March 1941 for further detail. See also Lt Gen Hans Baur, *Hitler's Pilot.*

EAGLE DAY

13 August 1940 saw one of the most decisive dates of the Battle. It is graphically described in Richard Collier's *Eagle Day*. *Adlerangriff* was meant to finish

Fighter Command for ever and to put paid to the RAF's dominance of the skies over the English Channel. Logically that is what should have happened. The Luftwaffe was more experienced, had greater numbers of both aircraft and men, and had the upper hand. But it was not to be. The weather was not in their favour, but though the main attack was postponed till the afternoon, some units were already on their way. Losses were great on both sides, but the victory went to Fighter Command. Meanwhile British bombers kept up the attack on the Luftwaffe's supply lines at night. For a full account see D. Wood and D. Dempster, *The Narrow Margin*; Len Deighton, *Fighter*; Drew Middleton, *The Sky Suspended*; Marcel Julian, *The Battle of Britain* (by one of France's leading writers on aerial warfare); and Alexander McKee, *Strike from the Sky*.

Five days later came what author Alfred Price calls *The Hardest Day*, 18 August 1940. This gives the regroupings of what followed Eagle Day and the disposition of the Luftwaffe units involved. Also listed are the losses for both sides, necessary maps and a good bibliography.

The following breakdown gives some idea of the scope of reading research when cross referenced with PRO records. These latter are itemised in the list of squadrons taking part in the Battle, and all are in the AIR 27 class index. Group records are in AIR 25 and Fighter Command in AIR 24.

Order of Battle of the Main Groups Involved on Eagle Day, 13 August 1940

10 Group, HQ Rudloe Manor, Box, Wiltshire. PRO Ref AIR 25/182–92. AOC: AVM Sir Christopher J. Quintin Brand.

SECTOR STATIONS

Pembrey: Wing Commander J. H. Hutchinson

92 Sqn	Sqn Ldr P. J. Sanders	Spitfire

Filton: Group Captain Robert Hanmer

87 Sqn	Sqn Ldr T. Lovell-Gregg	Hurricane
	Sqn Ldr R. S. Mills	
213 Sqn	Sqn Ldr H. D. McGregor	Hurricane
	Both 87 and 213 based at Exeter, then 87 to Bibury, 213 to Tangmere.	

St Eval: Fighter Section HQ: Group Captain L. G. le B. Croke

234 Sqn	Sqn Ldr J. S. O'Brien	Spitfire
	Flt Lt C. L. Page	
247 Sqn	Flt Lt G. F. Chater	
	One Flight only, from Roborough.	

11 Group, HQ Hillingdon House, Uxbridge, Middlesex. PRO Ref AIR 25/193–208. AOC: AVM Keith Rodney Park.

SECTOR STATIONS

Debden: Wing Commander Laurence Fuller-Good

17 Sqn	Sqn Ldr C. W. Williams	Hurricane
	Sqn Ldr A. G. Miller	
85 Sqn	Sqn Ldr Peter Townsend	

North Weald: Wing Commander Victor Beamish

56 Sqn	Sqn Ldr G. A. Manton	Hurricane
151 Sqn	Sqn Ldr J. A. Gordon	Hurricane
	Sqn Ldr Eric King	
	Sqn Ldr H. West	

Hornchurch: Wing Commander Cecil Bouchier

54 Sqn	Sqn Ldr James Leathart	Spitfire
	Sqn Ldr Donald Finlay	
	Sqn Ldr Pat Dunworth	
65 Sqn	Sqn Ldr A. L. Holland	Spitfire
74 Sqn	Sqn Ldr Francis White	Spitfire
	Sqn Ldr Adolph "Sailor" Malan	
266 Sqn	Sqn Ldr R. L. Wilkinson	
600 Sqn	Sqn Ldr David Clark	

Redhill, in the Hornchurch Sector, was a forward airfield for Kenley.

Biggin Hill: Group Captain Richard Grice

32 Sqn	Sqn Ldr John Worral	Hurricane
	Sqn Ldr Michael Crossley	
610 Sqn	Sqn Ldr John Ellis	Hurricane
501 Sqn	Sqn Ldr Harry Hogan	Hurricane

Hawkinge was a forward base to this sector under Sqn Ldr E. E. Arnold; also Lympne Sqn Ldr D. H. Montgomery.

Kenley: Wing Commander Tom Prickman

615 Sqn	Sqn Ldr Joseph Kayll	Hurricane
64 Sqn	Sqn Ldr Aeneas McDonell	Spitfire
111 Sqn	Sqn Ldr John Thompson	Hurricane
1 RCAF Sqn	Sqn Ldr Ernest McNab	Hurricane

Northolt: Group Captain Stanley Vincent

1 Sqn	Sqn Ldr D. A. Pemberton	Hurricane
303 Sqn	Sqn Ldr Zdzislaw Krasnodebski	
	Sqn Ldr Ronald Kellett	
257 Sqn	Flt Lt Robert Stanford-Tuck	Hurricane

Tangmere: Wing Commander Jack Boret

43 Sqn	Sqn Ldr John "Tubby" Badger	Hurricane
	Sqn Ldr Caesar Hull	
	Sqn Ldr Tom Dalton-Morgan	
145 Sqn	Sqn Ldr John Peel	Hurricane
601 Sqn	Sqn Ldr The Hon Edward Ward	Hurricane
	Flt Lt Sir Archibald Hope	

Middle Wallop: Wing Commander David Roberts

239 Sqn	Sqn Ldr Harold Fenton	Hurricane
	Flt Lt Minden Blake	
609 Sqn	Sqn Ldr Horace Darley	Spitfire
	Also from Warmwell under Wg Cdr George Howard.	
604 Sqn	Sqn Ldr Michael Anderson	Blenheim
152 Sqn	Sqn Ldr Peter Devitt	

Squadrons moved about a great deal from station to station, sometimes for only a few days, in order to give pilots a rest and to give the impression there were more squadrons than there actually were. A major part of the intention was to prevent identification; a moving target is less vulnerable than one associated with a particular place.

Books referring to some of these squadrons are listed separately, as are those relating to particular aircraft types. See also Perry Adams, *Hurricane Squadron*, about 87 Squadron; Frank H. Ziegler, *The Story of 609 Squadron: Under the White Rose*; and Roland Beamont, *My Part of the Sky*; Peter Townsend, *Duel of Eagles* and *Duel in the Dark*; I. Jones, *Tiger Squadron* (74 Sqn); Noel Monks, *Squadrons Up!* (1 and 73 Sqns); P.P.O. Sands, *Treble One* (111 Sqn). See also list of squadron histories by author on page 38.

11 Group's Operations Room is, of course, now disused. From here Sir Winston Churchill, PM, watched the last great aerial conflict of the Battle of Britain. It is preserved at RAF Uxbridge and may be seen by appointment. There is a reconstruction of it at the RAF Museum, Hendon, and photographs of it appear in many contemporary books. It was staffed mainly by WAAFs.

12 Group, HQ Watnall, Nr Nottingham, PRO Ref AIR 25/219. AOC: AVM Trafford Leigh-Mallory.

SECTOR STATIONS

Church Fenton: Group Captain C. F. Horsley

73 Sqn	Sqn Ldr M. W. Robinson	Hurricane
	Sqn Ldr Eric King	
	Sqn Ldr John Grandy	
616 Sqn	Sqn Ldr Marcus Robinson	Spitfire
	Sqn Ldr H. E. Burton	
302 Polish Sqn	Sqn Ldr Jack Satchell	Hurricane
	Sqn Ldr Mumler	

Kirton in Lindsey: Wing Commander S. H. Hardy

222 Sqn	Sqn Ldr Johnnie Hill	Spitfire
264 Sqn	Sqn Ldr Philip Hunter	Defiant
	Sqn Ldr Desmond Garvin	

Digby: Wing Commander Ian Parker

46 Sqn	Sqn Ldr J. R. MacLachlan	Hurricane

611 Sqn	Sqn Ldr James McComb	Spitfire
29 Sqn	Sqn Ldr S. C. Widdows	Blenheim

Coltishall: Wing Commander W. K. Beisegel

242 Sqn	Sqn Ldr Douglas Bader	Hurricane
66 Sqn	Sqn Ldr Rupert Leigh	Spitfire

Wittering: Wing Commander Harry Broadhurst

229 Sqn	Sqn Ldr H. J. Maguire	Hurricane
	Sqn Ldr John Banham	
23 Sqn	Sqn Ldr G. Heycock	Blenheim

Duxford: Wing Commander A. B. Woodhall

19 Sqn	Sqn Ldr P. C. Pinkham	Spitfire
	Sqn Ldr Bryan Lane	
	Also from Fowlmere satellite.	
310 Czech Sqn	Sqn Ldr Douglas Blackwood	Hurricane
	Sqn Ldr Sasha Hess	

11 and 12 Group were the main groups involved in the Battle, mainly over the London and Southeast areas. They were said to be rivals on the front line, their AOCs each jealously guarding his own territory. In reality all Groups pulled together, guarding the flanks of their neighbour and cooperating wherever necessary on the task in hand. It was, however, 11 Group which bore most of the brunt of the defence and attack and into which other fighter squadrons wished to become operational.

13 Group, HQ Blakelaw Estate, Ponteland Rd, Newcastle on Tyne. AOC: AVM Richard Ernest Saul. PRO Ref AIR 25/232.

SECTOR STATIONS

Catterick: Wing Commander G. L. Carter

219 Sqn	Sqn Ldr J. H. Little	Blenheim
41 Sqn	Sqn Ldr H.R.L. Hood	Spitfire

Usworth: Wing Commander Bryan Thynne — Fighter Sector HQ

607 Sqn	Sqn Ldr James Vick	Hurricane
72 Sqn	Sqn Ldr A. R. Collins	Spitfire
	Wg Cdr Ronald Lees	
	Flt Lt Edward Graham	
79 Sqn	Sqn Ldr Hervey Hayworth	Spitfire

Wick: Wing Commander Geoffrey Ambler — Fighter Section HQ
Coastal Command

3 Sqn	Sqn Ldr S. F. Godden	Hurricane
504 Sqn	Sqn Ldr John Sample	Hurricane
232 Sqn	Sqn Ldr M. M. Stephen	Hurricane
804 Fleet Air Arm Sqn, Coastal Command		

Dyce: Group Captain F. Crerar — Fighter Section HQ

Coastal Command		
603 Sqn	Sqn Ldr George Denholme	Spitfire
One Flight at Montrose.		
Turnhouse: Wing Commander the Duke of Hamilton		
605 Sqn	Sqn Ldr Walter Churchill	Hurricane
	Flt Lt Archie McKellar	
602 Sqn	Sqn Ldr "Sandy" Johnstone	
253 Sqn	Sqn Ldr Tom Gleave	Hurricane
	Sqn Ldr H. M. Starr	
	Sqn Ldr Gerry Edge	
141 Sqn	Sqn Ldr W. A. Richardson	Defiant
245 Sqn	Based at Aldergrove and administered from the Air Ministry	

See Sandy Johnstone, *Spitfire into Battle.*

These are the main groups and squadrons involved. For full Order of Battle and further detail see Richard Collier, *Eagle Day*, and Derek Wood and Derek Dempster, *The Narrow Margin.*

Their opposite numbers in the Luftwaffe, pilots, squadrons and bases, are listed in *Eagle Day* by Richard Collier.

To complete the rest of the year read *The Battle of Britain: The Forgotten Months, November–December 1940*, by John Foreman.

Coventry was bombed by 437 enemy aircraft on the night of 14/15 November 1940. The cathedral and much of the city were completely destroyed in Operation Moonlight Sonata.

Having failed in the attempt to destroy the RAF's Fighter Command and to bring the other services and civilians to their knees, Hitler temporarily withdrew from any further invasion attempt. The Luftwaffe's next task then was to destroy the will to resist on the ground. Thus it was intended to take away civilian support for the RAF by continuous bombing and false rumour. This was the period known as "the Blitz"—a short colloquialism from the German word *Blitzkrieg*, lightning war. That it failed to do either is another story. But read the novel *Blitz* for a factual, if fictional, account of the months that followed, written from the point of view of an American war-correspondent. It begins with the Battle of Britain.

POSTSCRIPT TO THE BATTLE

On 10/11 May 1941, another peace offer was made from Germany, by Rudolf Hess, who courageously and quixotically made the lone journey to Britain, landing by parachute from a crashing Messerschmitt near Glasgow in Scotland. He was not recognised immediately, having given a false name and it being believed this was well beyond a Messerschmitt's range. When taken to a hospital, it was supposed he was an ordinary Luftwaffe pilot who had strayed off course and was lost. Ostensibly he came to see the Duke of Hamilton, whom he claimed to have known in prewar days, with an offer from Hitler. The Duke, now Commanding Officer of 609 Squadron stationed at Turnhouse, was perplexed that he should have been singled out, as he had met Hess only once. He denied friendship, explaining he had been only one of several others to be introduced to Hitler's deputy. The offer, of course, meant total surrender, which was refused. The flight had required great courage to fly a single-seater unescorted aircraft, with only enough fuel for the journey, into the heartland of the enemy, and it must not be underestimated, especially in view of his continued postwar political captivity in Spandau.

The full story and the events leading up to that spring day serve as basic research in the following titles: James Douglas Hamilton, *Motive for a Mission*, and Wolf Rudiger Hess, *My Father, Rudolf Hess*. Read also the operations books of 609 Squadron and its base station Turnhouse, in the AIR 27 and AIR 28 series at the PRO, Kew. For War Office account, see WO 199/3288A—PRO, which includes the Duke's report.

THE THIRTY YEAR RULE

Until comparatively recently there was a closure period by which modern documents could not be seen by the general public until 50 years had elapsed since they were originally written and compiled. This has been reduced to 30 years, but it still means that original material may not be consulted within that thirty year period. Hence the name.

Material from the Second World War was not released until 1972. Some is still closed as being sensitive and is still not available from its top secret classification. Some of this still applies to certain categories of RAF material, but for the most part, that covering the Battle of Britain has been downgraded for public inspection.

This means that airmen writing of their own or other experiences before 1972 had no means of checking the facts other than from their own log books and memories and those of others in similar situations. Memory is not always as accurate as we think it is, and not everyone has total recall. This is not to say that personal experience is faulty, but now that the documents which would have aided the memories of such authors are available, it is as well to verify the facts, as the authors themselves would readily agree, and which many are now doing for their own satisfaction. Of course, not all operations books are accurate either—remember the conditions in which many of them were written—but they are the nearest we can come now to being there.

3

Miscellaneous Background Material: Maps, Squadrons, Groups, Air Classifications, Archival Material, the *London Gazette*

BADGES

ROYAL AIR FORCE
(Pilot's Wings)

A pilot could be an officer of any rank or a sergeant.

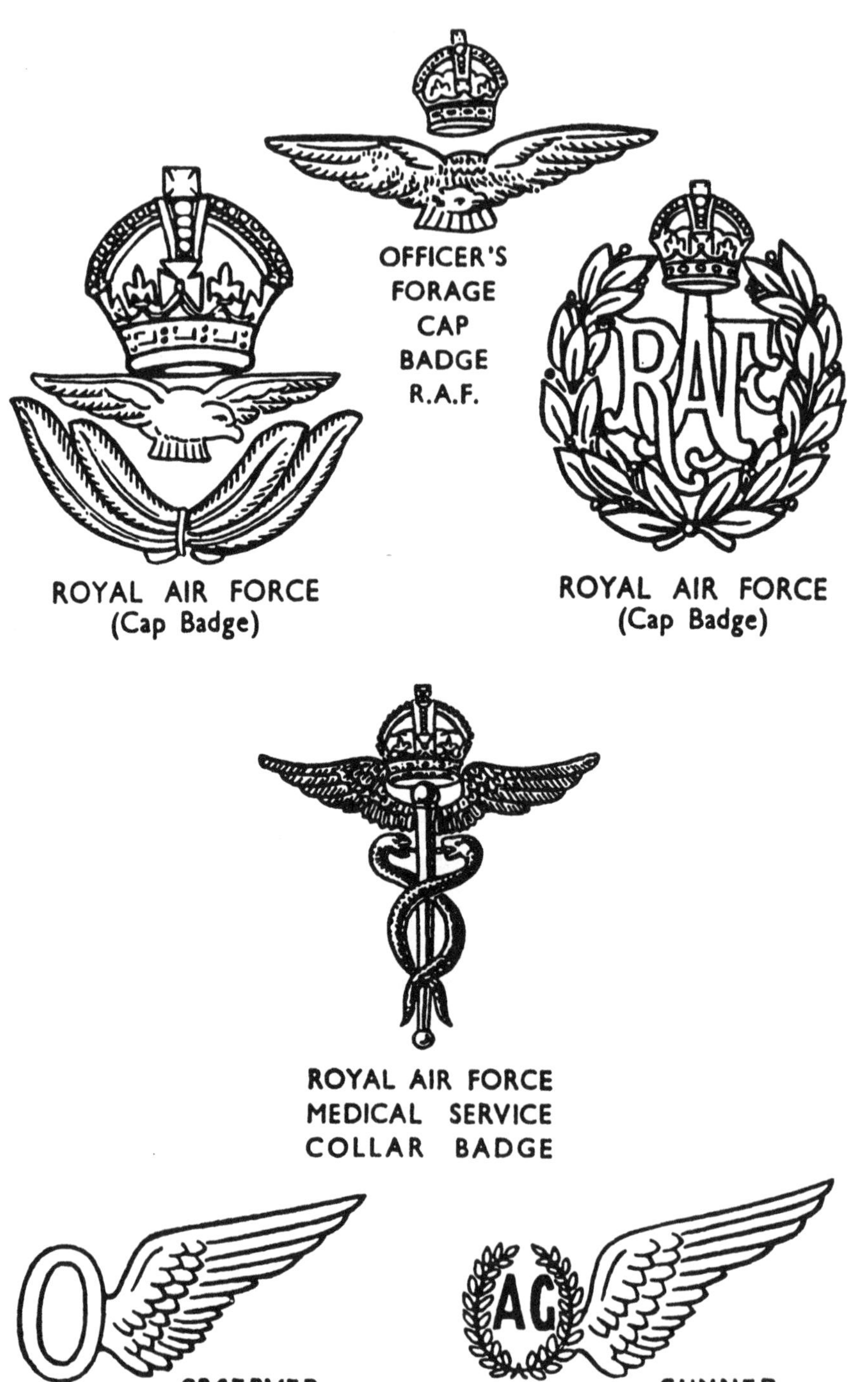

Cap badge worn by officers below air rank consists of the Crown, Eagle and Wreath. Officers of the WAAF and the Princess Mary's RAF Nursing Service wear a similar badge. Rankers and members of the Women's Auxiliary Air Force wear the monogram

DECORATIONS

Distinguished Flying Medal. Narrow stripes of dark bluish/purple running diagonally downward from right to left on a white ground. Awarded to non-commissioned officers and men in the same conditions as the DFC. A silver oval, with an effigy of the Sovereign on the obverse and on the reverse Athena Nike seated on an aeroplane. A hawk rises from her right hand above the words For Courage. Above the medal and attached to the clasp by wings is a bomb. The ribbon is 32 mm wide. The stripes were originally horizontal. The letters DFM are added to the recipient's name. Bars may be added for subsequent acts of courage, with a silver rose for undress uniform.

Distinguished Flying Cross. Established in June 1918 to be awarded to officers and warrant officers for acts of courage, valour, devotion to duty while flying in operations against the enemy. A silver cross flory, held at the horizontal and base bars by a bomb, the upper bar terminates in a winged rose surmounted by another cross composed of aeroplane propellers and a roundel within a wreath of laurels. The Imperial Crown carries the letters RAF. The reverse has the Royal cypher above the date 1918—the year the RAF was founded. It hangs from the 32 mm wide ribbon by two sprigs of laurel. The stripes are violet and white, wider but in the same diagonal as the DFM. The stripes were originally horizontal. The letters DFC are added after the recipient's name, bars are added for further acts and a silver rose with undress uniform.

Air Force Medal. Awarded to NCOs and men in the same conditions as the AFC. Oval, silver, the obverse is the same as the DFM. The reverse has a representation of Hermes mounted on a hawk bestowing a wreath. The stripes are as the DFM, but crimson and white. The letters AFM are added to the name.

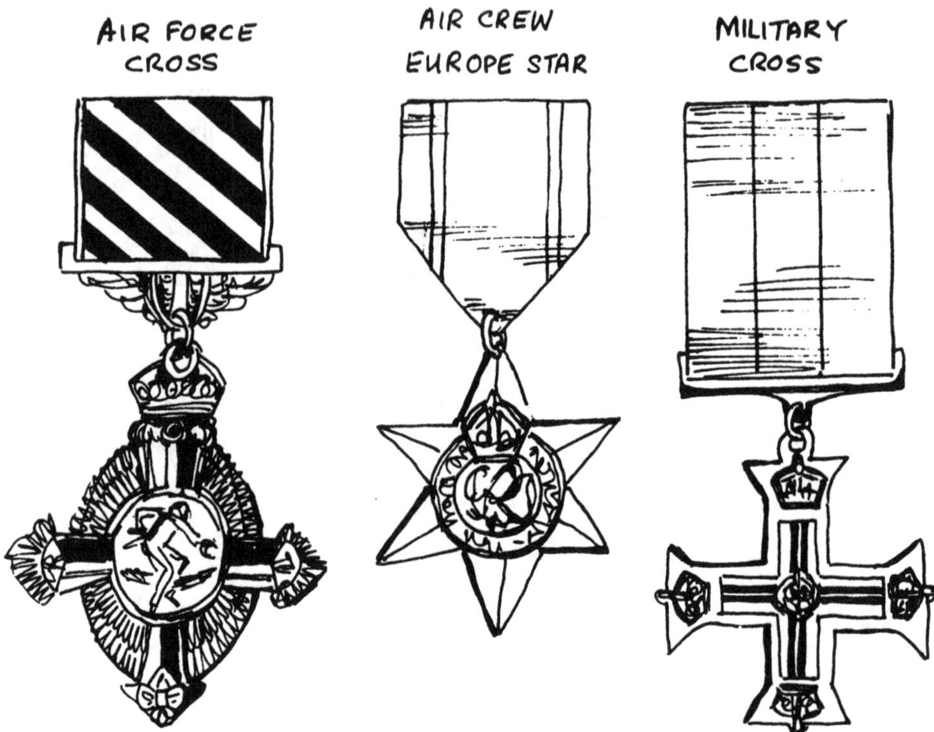

Air Force Cross. Awarded to officers and NCOs for an act of courage, valour, or devotion to duty while flying, though not on active operations against the enemy. It may also be awarded to individuals not in the air force who render distinguished service to aviation in actual flying. Silver, a thunderbolt in the form of a cross conjoined by the wings, base bar terminating in a bomb. These surmounted by another cross composed of propellers, four ends enscribed with the Royal cypher. The stripes are crimson and white, and the letters AFC are added to the recipient's name. In February 1970 the AFC was awarded for the first time to a naval officer.
Air Crew Europe Star. The 32 mm ribbon is pale blue with black edges and a narrow stripe either side the blue. This symbolises the day and night operations of air crew. Awarded for operational flying from UK bases over Europe and the UK for a period of two months from the outbreak of war on 3 September 1939 to 4 June 1944. Operations at sea was not a qualification. A bar or clasp indicates a second star.
Military Cross. Created in 1885, rewarding officers who have (1) completed twenty-five years good and loyal service as officers and (2) for twenty-five years service. The ribbon is green with a red stripe at each edge, and on it a rosette for the first class. The decoration is entirely in gold but the arms of the cross are in black.

MAPS AND DIAGRAMS

Southeast England, 1940

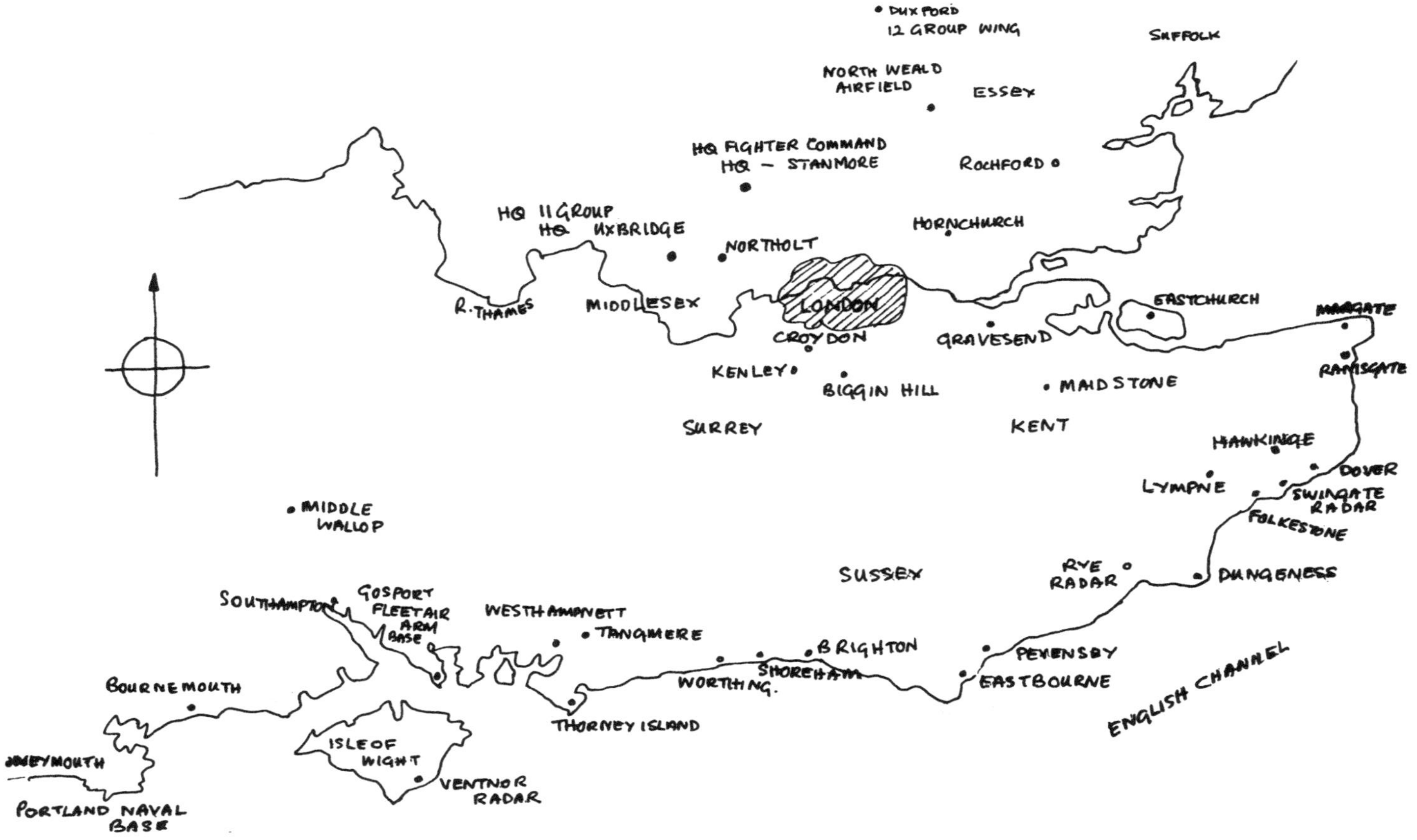

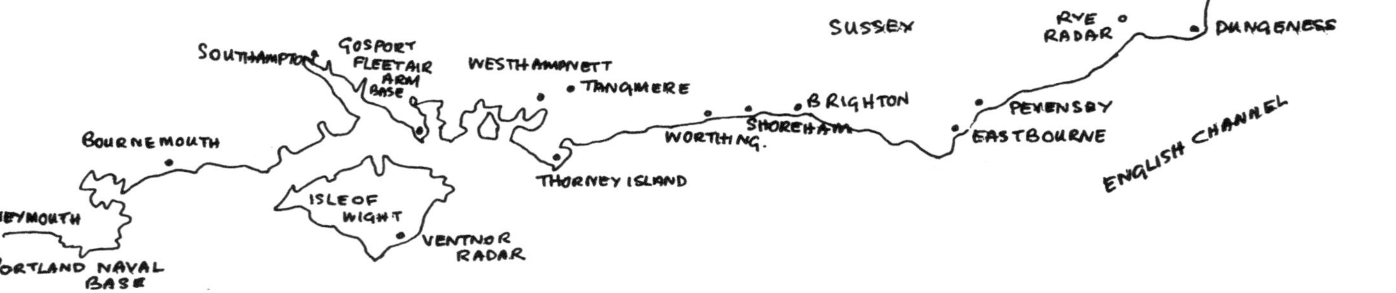

Fighter and Bomber Command Groups in the British Isles

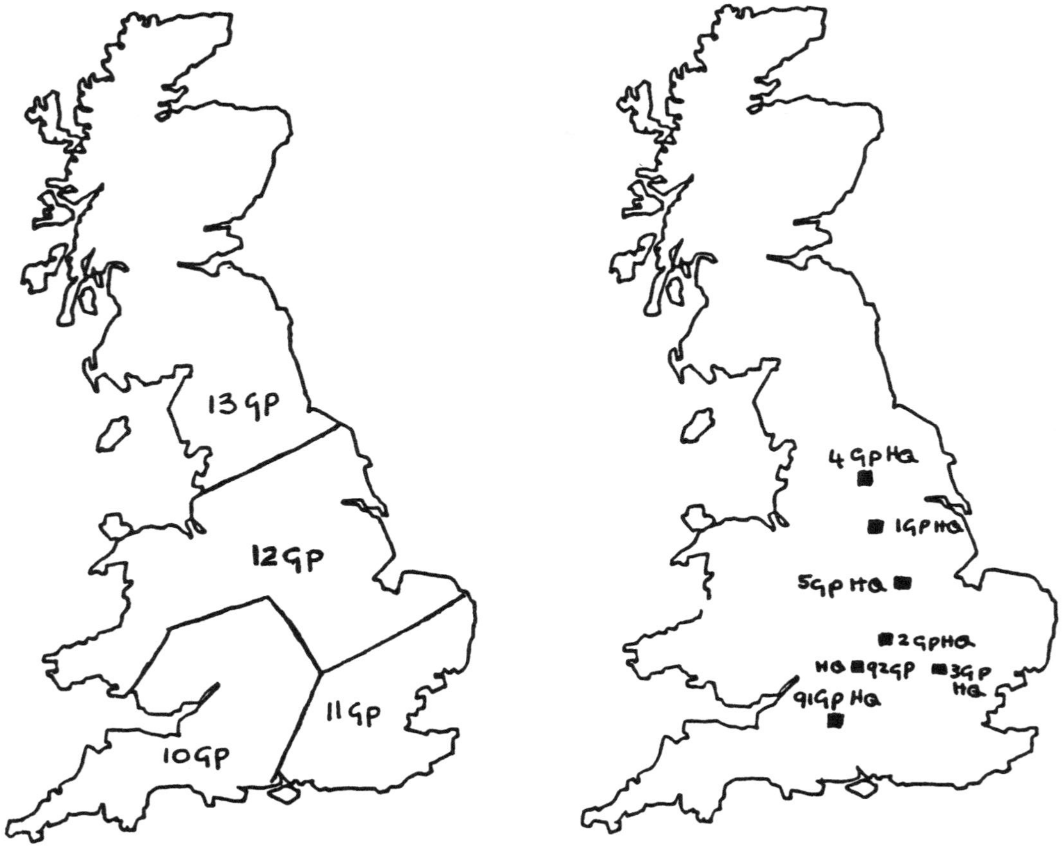

RAF Fighter Command Sectors and Group Boundaries

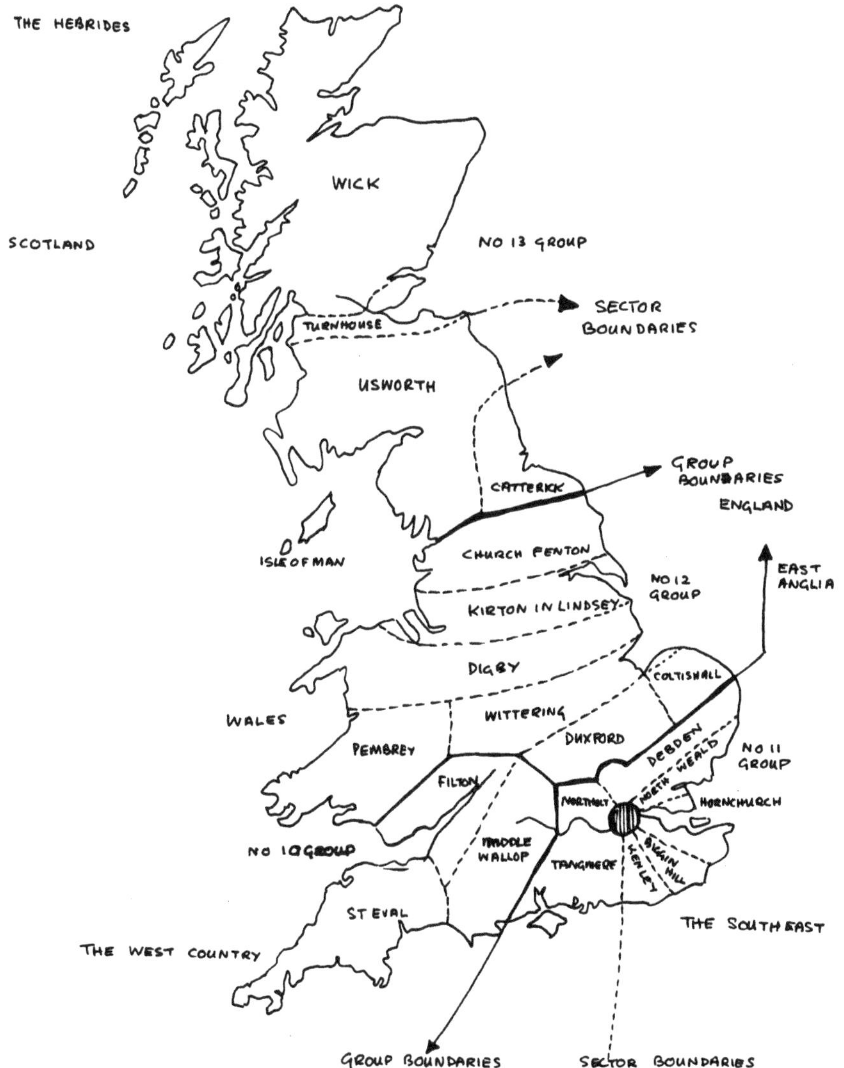

Divisions of Sectors

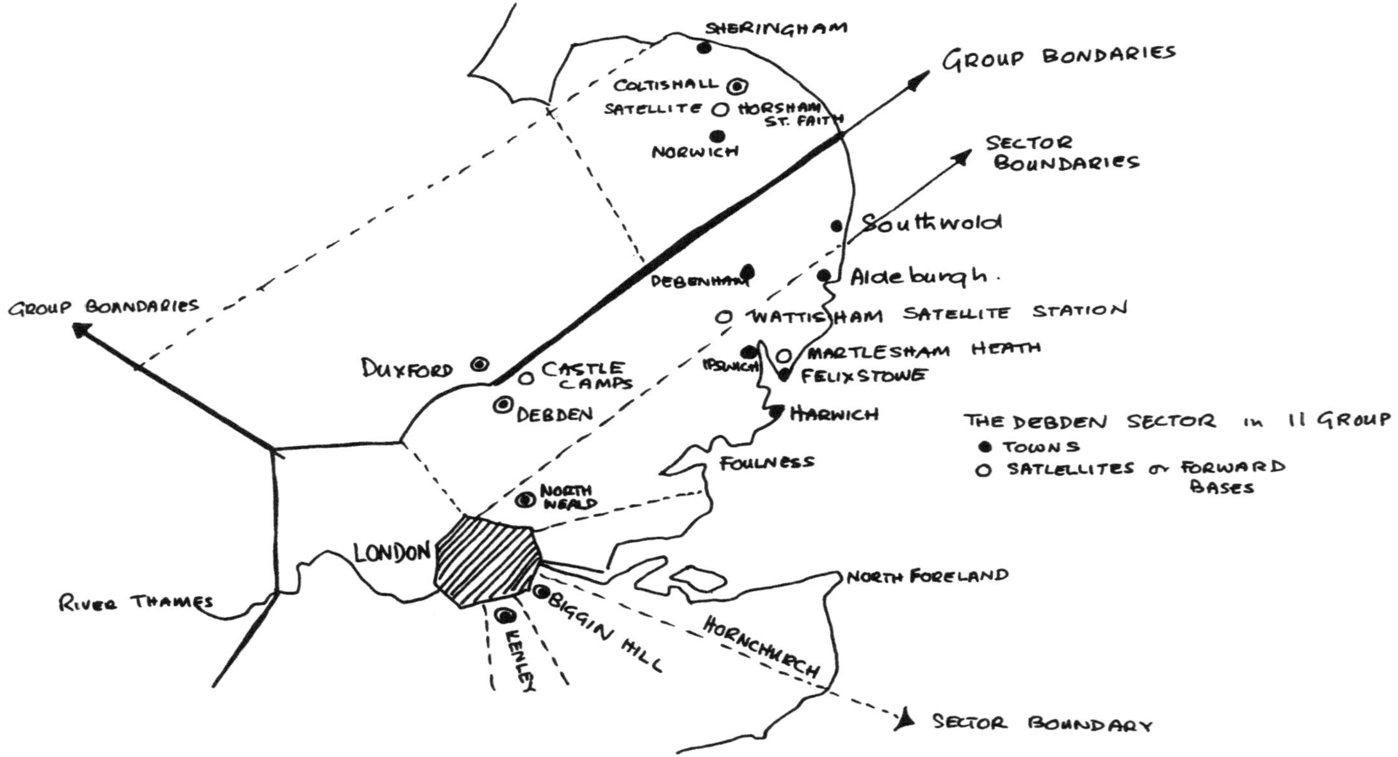

SHERINGHAM
GROUP BONDARIES
COLTISHALL
SATELLITE O HORSHAM ST. FAITH
NORWICH
SECTOR BOUNDARIES
Southwold
DEBENHAM
Aldeburgh.
GROUP BOANDARIES
O WATTISHAM SATELLITE STATION
IPSWICH
O MARTLESHAM HEATH
FELIXSTOWE
DUXFORD
O CASTLE CAMPS
DEBDEN
HARWICH
THE DEBDEN SECTOR in 11 GROUP
● TOWNS
O SATLELLITES or FORWARD BASES
FOULNESS
NORTH WEALD
LONDON
NORTH FORELAND
RIVER THAMES
BIGGIN HILL
KENLEY
HORNCHURCH
SECTOR BOUNDARY

Group Showing Sectors, London Defence

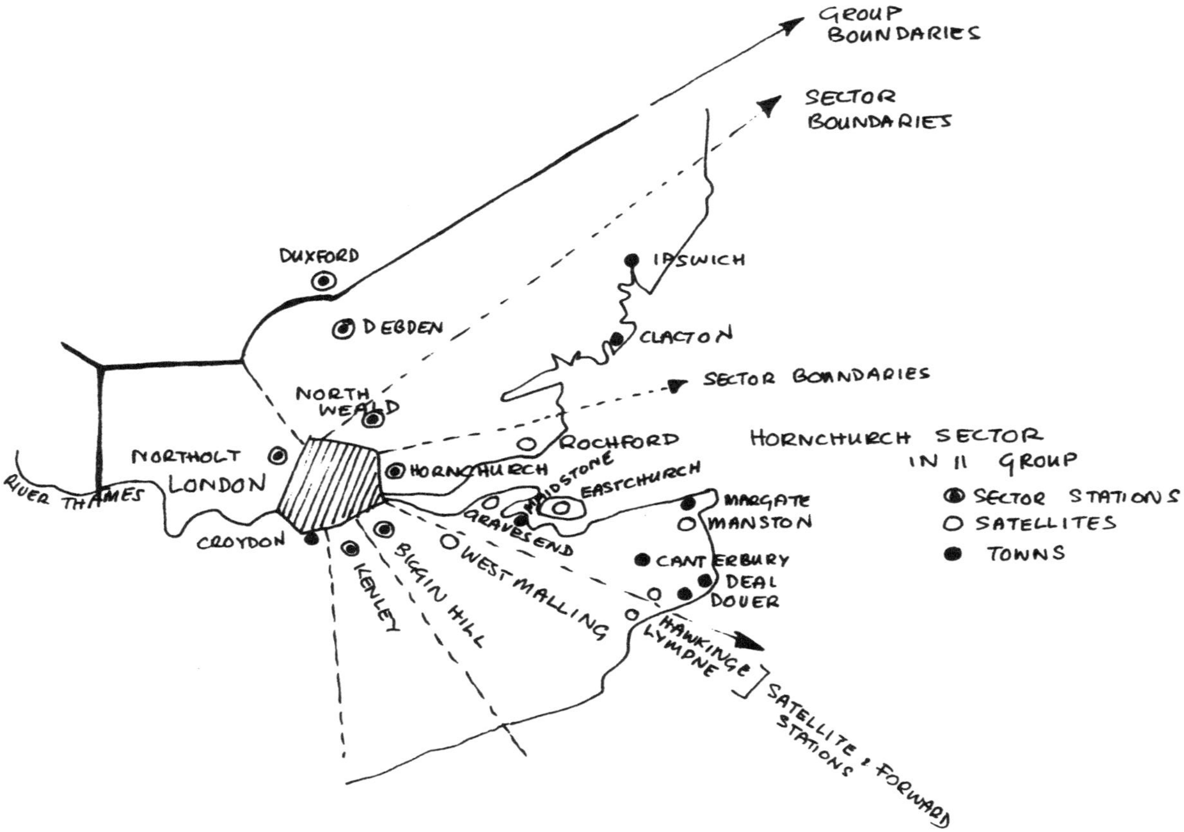

11 Group Showing Towns

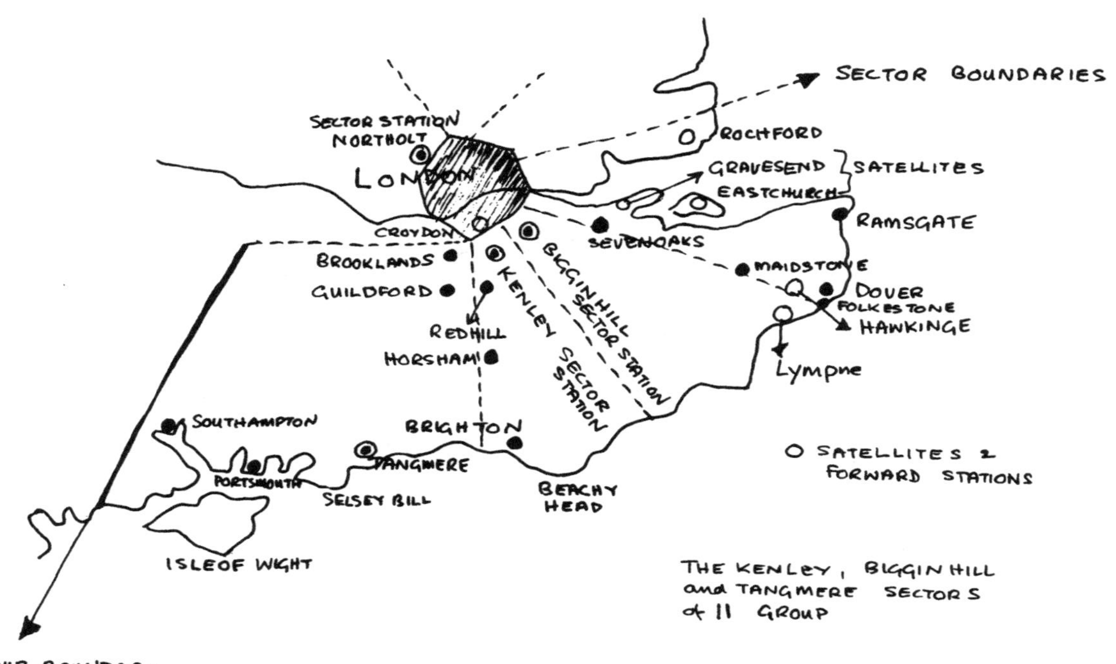

PRO RAF/AIR CLASSIFICATION LIST, NUMERICAL

Earlier background detail may be required, possibly from the following:

AIR 1	Air/min Registered Files 1914–
AIR 2	Air/min Registered Files up to 1934
AIR 2	Air/min Registered Files 1935–45 Air Historical Branch
AIR 3	Airship Log Books
AIR 4	Aircrew Log Books
AIR 5	Air Min Registered Files 1921 and WW2 Misc Papers AHB
AIR 6	Air Board and Air Council Records of Meetings
AIR 7	Personal Papers, Special
AIR 8	CAS (Chief of Staff)
AIR 9	Directorate of Plans
AIR 10	Air Publications, including Chief of Defence Staff and Senior Defence Staff
AIR 11	Airships, RAF Cardington, correspondence and papers
AIR 13	Balloon Command
AIR 14	Bomber Command
AIR 15	Coastal Command
AIR 16	Fighter Command inc. 60(s) and 88(s) Groups
AIR 17	Maintenance Command
AIR 18	J. A. G. Groups Martial Procedure
AIR 19	Private Office Papers
AIR 20	Unregistered Papers, Air Ministry HQ Branches
AIR 21	J. A. G. General Courts Martial Registers
AIR 22	Returns, Summaries and Bulletins, Periodic
AIR 23	Overseas Commands
AIR 24	ORBs—OPS BKS—Commands
AIR 25	ORBs Groups
AIR 27	Squadron Operational Record Books
AIR 28	Station Operational Record Books
AIR 28	Miscellaneous Units Operational Record Books
AIR 45	RAF Delegation, Washington 1935–45
AIR 46	UK Air Liaison Mission—Canada
AIR 47	Combined Planning Staff
AIR 48	U.S. Strategic Bombing Surveys
AIR 49	Medical Histories
AIR 50	Combat Reports

AIR 51	Allied Forces HQ Files Microfilm 1939–45
AIR 52	National Defence Research Committee USA
AIR 53	Home Command
AIR 54	STH African Air Force ORBs on microfilm
AIR 55	BAFO—Germany
AIR 56	HQ No. 90 SIGNALS—technical drawings
AIR 57	Direct General Medical Services—Flying Personnel Research Committee
AIR 58	Direct General Medical Services—Institute of Aviation Medicine
AIR 59	Directorate of Works—photographs
AIR 60	Directorate of Research—monthly reports 1919–25
AIR 62	Whittle Papers
AIR 63	Central Bomber Establishment
AIR 64	Central Fighter Establishment
AIR 65	Air/Sea Warfare Development Unit Reports

For entrance into the main areas of original document research see the list of squadron numbers in the "Squadrons Involved" section, below. This gives the Public Record Office reference for each squadron involved in AIR 27.

Most of AIR 27 is now on microfilm at the PRO as the originals are becoming too fragile to use. The compensation is that it is a help-yourself file and is therefore quicker to use. Check before ordering.

See also the "Order of Battle" in Chapter 2 for the Groups in which these squadrons operated, AIR 25, for a wider view of their activities.

In AIR 28 their operational stations or bases are indexed under their names. These books give ground operations and detail of what went on other than combat.

If the unit is known only by its description, e.g., Operational Training Unit or OTU, look in the index of AIR 29 under that description. Many RAF Regiment squadrons were involved in the Battle of Britain, in defending stations and bases, as well as manning Anti-Aircraft guns. These will be found also under their numbers in AIR 29.

Other archival material which may be used for cross referencing includes AIR 8, AIR 10, AIR 24, AIR 25—Groups, AIR 26—Wings, AIR 39—Army Co-operation, ADM 207—Fleet Air Arm, AVIA 15—Ministry of Aircraft Production, AVIA 20 and 15—Air Transport Auxiliary, civilians who ferried aircraft to and from factory to squadron, etc. Includes women pilots.

All these and more are described in the PRO leaflet 16, Research and Development of the RAF is in leaflet 47, Air Records as Sources for Biography and Family History, see leaflet 13. Prisoners of War in British hands or in Enemy hands, see leaflet 39. These leaflets may be asked for by post or in person from Public Record Office, Ruskin Avenue, Kew, Richmond, Surrey, UK.

ORIGINAL ARCHIVAL MATERIAL

Archival material is found mainly at the Public Record Office at Kew and at the RAF Museum, Hendon.

Operational Record Books, by squadron number, are located at the PRO in AIR 27.

Groups, by number, are in AIR 25. See also material listed in EVENTS 1940, for the groups, their commanding officers, and their order of battle.

Pilots' Log Books are in AIR 4, PRO. For example, AIR 4/7 Flt Lt A. Burnell-Phillips; 4/11 Sqn Ldr G. P. Christie; 4/17 F/O J. H. Coghlan; 4/19 W/Cdr W. E. Coope; 4/20 P/O J. L. Crisp; 4/21 Flt Lt D. M. Crooke, DFC; 4/32 Wg Cdr A. Eyre; 4/58 Sqn Ldr B.J.E. Lane; 4/77 P/O W. L. McKnight, DFC, and many others similar from the same period. This file is not complete, and not all logs will be found here. Aircrew were allowed to keep their logs after the war as their own personal property. Therefore some are still in private hands. Those not claimed after the cessation of hostilities were advertised so that next of kin could claim them. Those not so claimed were destroyed. Those in the archive are representative, but do not expect them to be sensational writings. There are others at the RAF Museum, Hendon, and occasionally logs turn up in auctions and book sales.

Logs of others who were not pilots, including miscellaneous aircrew, aircrew under training, and other ranks might offer personal and immediate background. Those lodged at the PRO might be there through being donated after death by the airman's family, or by the owner himself. That of Paddy Finucane is a photocopy donated by his family. It is worth studying for the contrast it offers in the length of time in training of a prewar pilot—Finucane joined the RAF in 1938. Read this alongside Doug Stokes's *Paddy Finucane: Fighter Ace* (a block of flats in Richmond, Surrey, where Finucane lived, is named in his memory). *The Second World War: A Guide to the Records at the Public Record Office*, published by HMSO in 1972, is, though not specifically about the Battle of Britain, a considerable help as to what can be found and where about this and any other related period.

THE *LONDON GAZETTE* (PRO/Kew Reference ZJI/----)

This was a printed document issued monthly from 1665, and up to 1984 is available at the PRO at the time of writing. The index is to be found on the open shelves. There is also a full run at the British Library. The first few years of the 1600s are in French.

For the war years this is the nearest we can get to a Muster Roll of the RAF, but it contains much other valuable service and civilian information on commissionings, promotions of officers, decorations and awards as well as mentions in despatches of other ranks including NCOs. 1940 runs from ZJI/932 to 943, with earlier and later years similarly listed. There is a separate number for each month; those with asterisks indicate an index for the previous quarter. References are by page number.

1940	January	ZJI/932
	February	933
	March*	934
	April	935
	May	936
	June*	937
	July	938
	August	939
	September*	940
	October	941
	November	942
	December*	943

Awards and citations carry the recipient's name, rank, number and squadron. Example: F/O Paul Henry Mills Richey, 39757, DFC, 5 Nov 1940, No 1 Squadron, for gallantry and devotion to duty in the exercise of air operations.

Service numbers only are given in the promotions lists, enabling other details to be tracked by relatives only, through RAF Innsworth, the RAF's Record Office. WAAFs are included. In the case of promotion from NCO or other rank, existing airman number is given as well as that of commission. Example: D. J. Renvoize, page 6398—numbers 748534/86338, 14 September 1940 from sergeant to commission.

The only General Muster Roll was made when the RFC became the RAF on 1 April 1918. It is in service number order, so unless this is known cannot be searched by name. There is no other for the modern RAF, but Nominal Rolls can occasionally found in the station records when a whole unit, not just a squadron, moved from one place to another. If found, these will be in AIR 28 or 29, and the station described by name.

SQUADRONS INVOLVED (PRO Reference Numbers)

The task of squadron research is made easier if the total number involved and the corresponding reference to their operational books at the PRO are known. These reference numbers, following the class reference AIR 27, may vary according to the year.

Squadron No.	Aircraft	Operational Book PRO Reference
1	Hurricane	AIR 27/1 & 2
3	Hurricane	32 & 33
17	Hurricane	234
19	Spitfire	252–53
23	Blenheim	287
25	Blenheim	305
29	Blenheim	341
32	Hurricane	60–61
41	Spitfire	424–25
43	Hurricane	441
46	Hurricane	460
54	Spitfire	511
56	Hurricane	528
64	Spitfire	589
65	Spitfire	592
66	Spitfire	598
72	Spitfire	624
73	Hurricane	629
74	Spitfire	640
79	Hurricane	664
85	Hurricane	703
87	Hurricane	712
92	Spitfire	743
111	Hurricane	866
141	Hurricane	969
145	Hurricane	984
151	Hurricane	1018
152	Spitfire	1025
213	Hurricane	1315
219	Blenheim	1354
222	Spitfire	1371
229	Hurricane	1418
232	Hurricane	1428
234	Spitfire	1439
235	Blenheim	1442
236	Blenheim	1445

238	Hurricane	1453
245	Hurricane	1481
247	Gladiator	1487
248	Blenheim	1495
249	Hurricane	1498
253	Hurricane	1511
257	Hurricane	1526

SQUADRON HISTORIES BY NUMBER: GENERAL SURVEY

Every squadron, including those of the Commonwealth and Allies, fighter and bomber, or with other functions, is listed in the AIR 27 Class at the Public Record Office. Some were resurrected numbers from the RFC; some have a continuous history from that period. Others from time to time are renumbered or amalgamated. The operations books (ORBs) are each squadron's official diary and history. There are several books which list these squadrons with their dates, equipment, location, and so on and are a summarised history of the unit. Starting points are Chris Ashworth, *Encyclopedia of Modern Royal Air Force Squadrons*; (Wellingborough: Patrick Stephens, 1989. Sixty-seven present-day squadrons and their histories. Illustrated badges, battle honours, mascots, banners and memorials. Good photographs. Author was in RAF for 32 years); James Halley, *The Squadrons of the RAF* (Tonbridge: Air Britain, 1988. Revised and updated frequently. Similar potted histories of RAF squadrons including those disbanded.); Wg Cdr C. G. Jefford, *Royal Air Force Squadrons* (Shrewsbury: Airlife, 1987. A comprehensive record of all RAF squadrons and their antecedents since 1912); and Anthony Robinson, *RAF Fighter Squadrons in the Battle of Britain* (London: Arms and Armour Press, 1988). All are essential reference reading for serious researchers.

SQUADRON HISTORIES BY AUTHOR

For publisher, date, and further detail, see author section. Perry Adams, *Hurricane Squadron* (87 Squadron); Anthony Bartley, *Smoke Trails in the Sky* (92 Squadron); James Beedle, *History of the Fighting Cocks* (43 Squadron); Belgian Air Force Squadron 11, Fl Lt D. M. Crook, *Spitfire Pilot* (609 Squadron); J. L. Dixon, *In All Things First* (1 Squadron); A. Fiedler, *Polish Fighter Squadron* (303 Squadron); John Freeman, *The Forgotten Months*; Norman Franks, *Sky Tiger* (74 Squadron), *Valiant Wings* (Battle and Blenheim Squadrons in France, AASF, 1939–40); James Halley, *Squadrons of the RAF*; HMSO, *Great Britain, 92 Squadron, Great Britain, 111 Squadron, Short History of 151 Squadron, Short History of 213 Squadron*; Wg Cdr C. G. Jefford, *Squadrons of the RAF*; Wg Cdr Ira Jones, *Tiger Squadron* (74 Squadron); A. S. Kennedy, *City of Edin-*

burgh's Fighter Squadron (603 Squadron); Sqn Ldr M. A. Liskutin, *Challenge in the Air* (145, 312, 313 Squadrons); Noel Monks, *Squadrons Up*! (1 and 73 Squadron); Tom Moulson, *The Flying Sword* (601 Squadron); F. G. Nancarrow, *Glasgow's Fighter Squadron* (602 Squadron); Jeffrey Quill, *Spitfire: A Test Pilot's Story* (65 Squadron included); G. F. Rawnsley and Robert Wright, *Night Fighter* (604 Squadron); Anthony Robinson, *RAF Fighter Squadrons in the Battle of Britain*; Fl Lt W. T. Rolls, *Spitfire Attack* (72 Squadron); Fg Off R.P.D. Sands, *Treble One* (111 Squadron); Michael Shaw, *Twice Vertical* (1 Squadron); Douglas Tidy, *I Fear No Man* (74 Squadron); Frank Ziegler, *Under the White Rose* (609 Squadron).

See also the following articles: *Daily Express* "54 Squadron, The Fighting Fifty-Fourth" (14–15 August 1950). F/O Smith, their Intelligence Officer wrote, "truly amazing pilots"; *Life*, 24 June 1940; *Sunday Express* "The Fighter Pilot and His Type" (21 July 1940).

SQUADRON PROFILES

These are histories of individual squadrons or factual stories by people who served in them. Check by number against the operational record in PRO reference AIR 27. For full information, see author section.

1 Squadron: J. L. Dixon, *In All Things First*; Noel Monks, *Squadrons Up*! (dedicated to New Zealand's top flying Ace, Cobber Kain); Michael Shaw, *Twice Vertical* and *No. 1 Squadron.*

43 Squadron: James Beedle, *43 Squadron RFC-RAF, the History of the Fighting Cocks, 1916–1966.*

65 Squadron: Jeffrey Quill, *Spitfire: A Test Pilot's Story.*

72 Squadron: Flt Lt W. T. Rolls, *Spitfire Attack.*

73 Squadron: Noel Monks, *Squadrons Up*!

74 Squadron: Wg Cdr Ira "Taffy" Jones, *Tiger Squadron*; Douglas Tidy, *I Fear No Man, RFC and RAF*; Norman Franks, *Sky Tiger.*

87 Squadron: Perry Adams, *Hurricane Squadron—87 Squadron at War, 1939–1941*

85 Squadron: Flt Lt P. Warren, *RAF West Raynham.*

92 Squadron: Sqn Ldr Anthony F. Bartley, DFC, *Smoke Trails in the Sky.*

103 Squadron: Sid Finn, *Black Swan.*

111 Squadron: P.P.O. Sands, *Treble One.*

233 Squadron: Gron Edwards, *Norwegian Patrol.*

242 Squadron: A.E.M. Barton, *242 Squadron.*

247 Squadron: Wg Cdr K. W. Mackenzie, DFC, AFC, *Hurricane Combat.* See also 501 Squadron.

303 Squadron: Arkady Fiedler, *303 Polish Fighter Squadron*; Gp Capt J. A. Kent, *One of the Few.*

488 NZ Squadron: Leslie Hunt, *Defence until Dawn.*

501 Squadron: R. Aux, A. F., *Fear Nothing*; Wg Cdr K. W. Mackenzie, DFC, AFC, *Hurricane Combat.* See also 247 Squadron.

601 Squadron: Tom Moulson, *The Flying Sword.*

602 Squadron: F. G. Nancarrow, *Glasgow's Fighter Squadron*; AVM Sandy Johnstone, CB DFC AE, *Spitfire into Battle*; Douglas McRoberts, *Lions Rampant.*

603 Squadron: A. Scott Kennedy, *City of Edinburgh's Fighter Squadron*, and *Gin Ye Daur* (If You Dare).

604 Squadron: C. F. Rawnsley and Robert Wright, *Night Fighter.*

609 Squadron: Frank Ziegler, *The Story of 609 Squadron: Under the White Rose*; Flt Lt D. M. Crook, Spitfire Pilot.

Fictitious Squadron: Derek Robinson, *Piece of Cake* (also TV film, 1988).

See also Peter Lewis, *Squadron Histories 1–695*; James Halley, *The Squadrons of the Royal Air Force*; Wg Cdr C. G. Jefford, MBE, *Squadrons of the Royal Air Force*; Leslie Hunt, *21 Squadrons: History of the Royal Auxiliary Air Force*; A. V. Robertson, *Squadrons of the RAF*; J.D.R. Rawlings, *Fighter Squadrons of the RAF.*

4

Subject Listing

ABBREVIATIONS

Many good reference books contain lists of the common abbreviations and initials used in and about the Service. Of these, the list in C. H. Ward-Jackson's *Airman's Song Book* is the most comprehensive. Some are also found in his book *It's a Piece of Cake* and in the following:

The Action Stations series. Various authors. Wellingborough: Patrick Stephens.

Pretz, Bernard. *Dictionary of Military and Technological Abbreviations and Acronyms.* London: Routledge and Kegan Paul, 1983. Copy at PRO.

Smith, David J. *Britain's Military Airfields, 1939–45.* Wellingborough: Patrick Stephens, 1989.

Terraine, John. *The Right of the Line.* London: Hodder and Stoughton, 1985; Sceptre, 1988. This book is invaluable for many reference reasons.

AIRCRAFT

Andrews, C. F., and E. B. Morgan. *Supermarine Aircraft Since 1914.* London: Putnam, 1987.

———. *Vickers Aircraft Since 1908.* London: Putnam, 1989.

Bowyer, Chaz. *Hurricane at War.* London: Ian Allan, 1975.

Chinnery, Phil. *Gate Guards.* Manchester: World Books.

Emory, John. *Source Book of World War II Aircraft.* Poole, Dorset: Blandford Press.

Jackson, P. A. *French Military Aircraft.* Directory of individual aircraft details.

Lloyd, F.H.M. *Hurricane: The Story of a Great Fighter.* Harborough: Harborough Publishing, 1945.

Mason, Frank. *The Hawker Hurricane*. Bourne End: Aston House, 1987.
———. *Hawker Typhoon and Tempest*. Bourne End: Aston House, 1989.
Mole, Gp Capt Edward. *Happy Landings*. Wessex Aircraft.
Monday, David, ed. *Complete Illustrated Encyclopedia of the World's Aircraft*. London.
Morgan, Eric, and Edward Shacklady. *Spitfire, the History*. Stamford, Lincs: Guild Publishing and Key Publishing, 1987. The ultimate Spitfire reference book.
Price, Alfred. *Spitfire at War*. London: Ian Allan, 1974, 1985.
Rouse, Wally. *Born Again—Spitfire PS915*. Earl Shilton, Leicesters: Midlands Counties Publications, 1989.
Stewart, Adrian. *Hurricane*. London: William Kimber, 1982.
Sturtivant, Ray. *The Anson File*. Saffron Walden, Essex: Air Britain, 1988. Airtaxi of the RAF. 14,000 entries.

AIR DEFENCE OF GREAT BRITAIN

This was a general use of words describing the RAF's peacetime role at home before the war of 1939, the weakness of which was clearly outlined in Lord Dowding's warnings to the government. Loosely used as ADGB, it is also described as Southern Command, for which the Hendon Air Display and the Aldershot Tattoo were the shop windows. The ADGB remained when the RAF became the Air Component in France with the British Expeditionary Force (BEF). For description see:

Richards, Dennis. *Portal of Hungerford*. London: Heinemann, 1977.
Terraine, John. *The Right of the Line*. London: Hodder and Stoughton, 1985.

See also at the PRO the six volumes of *The Air Defence of Great Britain*: Vol. 1, AIR 41/14, 1936–40; Vol. 2, AIR 41/15, The Battle of Britain; Vol. 3, AIR 41/17, June 1940–41; Vol. 4, AIR 41/18, 1940–41; Vol. 5, AIR 41/19; Vol. 6, AIR 41/55.

Collier, Basil. *Defence of the United Kingdom*. London: HMSO, 1957.
Ellis, John. *Social History of the Machine Gun*. London: Croom Helm.
Powers, Barry D. *British Air Defence 1914–1939*. Texas, 1976.

See also other books of a general content about the RAF, including those of a biographical nature, such as Vincent Orange, *Sir Keith Park*, which has excellent chapter notes, a detailed bibliography of published and unpublished sources, and a good index. This volume describes the HQ ADGB at Uxbridge. Uxbridge is still an RAF Station on the outskirts of London, to which many airmen remember being sent for their first kitting out and introduction to RAF life. Permission to see the Control Room may be sought from the Commanding Officer.

ADGB was part of the RAF as formed in 1918, but on 14 July 1936 was disolved and became RAF Fighter Command with its AOC, Sir Hugh Dowding. There were four domestic formations, 11 and 12 Groups, Fighters, 22 Group Army Co-operation, and the civilian Observer Corps whose job it was to give advance warning. This arrangement remained until after the Battle of Britain and until the Second Tactical Airforce was formed for the Normandy invasion. Material for ADGB will therefore be found in many different PRO classes, not necessarily all in AIR Indexes.

AIRFIELDS

For an initial and general study of airfields in the UK, the Action Stations series should first be consulted. Compare these named stations with AIR 28 and 29 at the PRO for operational details. Many presently operating RAF stations hold Open Days, some especially timed to celebrate Battle of Britain Wings Week. Among these is that at North Weald which holds an AIR Tattoo. A booklet published in 1971 is especially useful in telling their history.

The publisher's lists of Airfield Research Publications is also worth consulting. See J. B. Thompson's *Charter Hall* (New Malden, 1989), where the badly burned Battle of Britain pilot, Richard Hillary, was killed. Hillary's papers are at Trinity College, Cambridge.

Other airfields which have local airports, such as Exeter, have produced their own titles—such as *Exeter Airport in Peace and War from 1938.*

Bowyer, Michael J. F. *Duxford: Its First Year of War.* East Anglian Aviation Society, 1974.

Brooks, R. J. *From Moths to Merlins: The Story of West Malling.* Battle of Britain station, 1930s–1980s.

Butler, P. H., ed. *British Isles, Airfield Guide.* Liverpool: Merseyside Aviation Society, 1976.

"Chiefy" B. (pseud.). "Goings On." RAF Gravesend, 1973.

Copeman, Geoff. *Silksheen.* 1989. Lincoln's airfield, 57 and 630 Sqns.

Corbell, Peter. "RAF Hornchurch." *Air Britain Digest* 3, nos. 9, 10 (from 1938, updated).

Fraser, F/O W. *Manston, the Story of the RAF Station.* Station history information handbook. Littlebury & Co, 1973.

Halpenny, B.B. *To Shatter the Sky.* Wellingborough: Patrick Stephens. Lincolnshire and Yorkshire, WW2. Also Film script, 1984.

Kinsey, Gordon. *Bawdsey.* Lavenham: Terence Dalton, 1983.

———. *Martlesham Heath, 1917–1973.* Lavenham: Terence Dalton, 1983.

———. *Orfordness, 1915–80.* Lavenham: Terence Dalton, 1986.

Promise and Fulfill: 50 Years of the RAF at Odiham. Bird Brothers, 1974. Information handbook, Constitutional Press, 1974.

Smith, David J. *Britain's Military Airfields, 1939–45.* Wellingborough: Patrick Stephens, 1989. Good bibliography and abbreviations list.

Sutton, Sqn Ldr H.T. *Raiders Approach.* Aldershot: Gale and Polden, 1956. RAF Hornchurch and Sutton's Farm.

Thompson, J.B. *Charter Hall.* New Malden, Surrey: Airfield Research Publications, 1989.

Wallace, Graham. *Biggin Hill, 1917–1954.* London: Putnam, 1957. Reprint, London: Tandem, 1975. Station history. London's famous fighter station. Now closed as an RAF Station, but the chapel can be seen with permission from the guardroom.

Willis, Steve, and Barry Hollis. *Military Airfields of the British Isles*. Originally in three volumes on open shelves at the PRO, now in one omnibus edition. Kettering: authors, 1988.

Headquarters, Non-Flying

Bentley Priory. Constitutional Press, 1974. HQ 11 Group, Stanmore Park. Information handbook.

Escott, Sqn Ldr Beryl E. *RAF High Wycombe*. Constitutional Press, 1974.

RAF High Wycombe. Constitutional Press, 1974.

RAF Northolt. Constitutional Press, 1974. Information handbook.

RAF Stanmore Park. Constitutional Press, 1974.

RAF Uxbridge. Constitutional Press, Littlebury & Co., 1969. Central information booklet.

AIRFIELDS INVOLVED IN THE BATTLE OF BRITAIN

The Action Stations Series should first be consulted for the relevant dates. There are also many local aviation societies which study and research aviation in their area. Addresses are available from local reference or local studies libraries.

Bowyer, Michael J.F. *Duxford: Its First Year of War*. Duxford, Cambridgeshire: East Anglian Aviation Society, 1974.

Butler, P.H., ed. *British Isles, Airfield Guide*. Liverpool: Merseyside Aviation Society, 1976.

"Chiefy" B (pseud.). *RAF Gravesend "Goings On."* RAF Gravesend, 1973.

Cluett, Douglas, J. Bogle, and B. Learmouth. *The Battle for Britain*, vol. 3. Sutton Public Libraries, 1985.

———. *The First Croydon Airport, 1915–28*. Sutton Public Libraries.

———. *1928–39, the Great Days*. Vol. 2. Sutton Public Libraries.

Cooksley, Peter G. *Croydon Airport Fly Past*. London: Robert Hale, 1983. Has color profiles of aircraft.

Corbell, Peter. "RAF Hornchurch." *Air Britain Digest* 3, nos. 9, 10.

Fraser, F/O W. *Manston, the Story of the RAF Station: Station History, 1972*. Littlebury and Co., 1973. Information handbook.

Kinsey, Gordon. *Martlesham Heath, 1917–73*. Lavenham: Terence Dalton, 1963.

Odiham, Information handbook. Constitutional Press, 1974.

Orange, Vincent. *The Road to Biggin Hill*. Shrewsbury: Air Life, 1986.

Promise and Fulfill, RAF Odiham: 50 Years of the RAF at Odiham. Bird Brothers, 1975.

Sutton, Sqn Ldr H.T. *Raiders Approach*! Aldershot: Gale and Polden, 1956. RAF Hornchurch and Sutton's Farm.

Tangmere Military Aviation Museum (near Chichester). The Guide Booklet and others are available at the shop on site, or by post. Not available elsewhere.

Wallace, Graham. *Biggin Hill*. London: Putnam, 1957. Reprint. London: Tadem, 1975. Britain's most famous fighter station, Station history.

Many airfields were temporary landing grounds, such as at Funtington, and do not now exist as such, nor is there specific literature about them. But most are mentioned in the Action Stations Series and in local history collections in libraries and county record offices. As well, and importantly, all these air stations can be checked out via their operations books in AIR 28 and 29 at the PRO. Some, such as at Hurn, now Bournemouth's busy civil airport, and Ford, an open prison, have changed their function and can be found in local record offices. Others are private property, returned to the farmers, and permission should be sought before entering.

THE AIR TRANSPORT AUXILIARY (ATA)

The ATA was a civilian organisation formed to relieve service pilots for active duty by ferrying all aircraft types to and from the factories, squadrons and units. Members wore navy blue uniforms with gold braid and wings, and all had considerable flying or engineering experience. Many were women who were not admitted as pilots into the RAF; some were over age men who were not British and as such not accepted by the RAF; others were medically unfit. Many were Americans.

The Ferry Pool and ATA HQ was at White Waltham in 41 Group and its records are in the PRO in AVIA 27/1 and 2, 5–6–7 as well as in AVIA 2 and 15. See also records in AIR 20/456.

Personnel may also be found in AVIA 81, but AVIA 74 is not yet at the PRO.

WAAFs (Womens Auxiliary Air Force) who wanted to transfer to the ATA as pilots may be found in AIR 2/6092.

The ATA Association's address is at 40 Goldcrest Rd., Chipping Sodbury, Bristol BS17 6XG. The ATA Memorial is in St Paul's Cathedral, London.

Other works about the ATA include Jackie Moggeridge's *Woman Pilot* (London: Michael Joseph, 1957; London: Pan Books, 1959), and Lettice Curtis's *The Forgotten Pilots* (Olney: Nelson and Saunders, 1971).

AMERICANS IN THE RAF (BATTLE OF BRITAIN)

The three Eagle Squadrons in the RAF were 71, 121 and 133, all to be found in AIR 27 at the PRO, their operations books and by base name in AIR 28. Only 71 was formed early enough to take part in the Battle, but other Americans are often found in RAF squadrons or under training in OTUs (Operational Training Units), often with RCAF after their names, if before November 1941. They were all volunteers and risked losing their citizenship by joining the armed forces of a foreign country when their own country was not at war.

Boebert, Earl. "The Eagle Squadrons." *American Aviation Historical Society Journal* (Spring 1964).

Donahue, Art. *Tally Ho! Yankee in a Spitfire.* London: Macmillan, 1943.
Haughland, Vern. *The Eagle Squadrons: Yanks in the RAF, 1940–42.* Newton Abbot: David and Charles, 1979.
———. *The Eagles' War.* New York: Jason Aronson, 1982.
Hawkins, Leslie Brampton. *Eagle Squadron Remembered.* London: Excalibur Press, 1990. Poems dedicated to the Eagle Squadron, 1938–45.
Victor, John A. *Time Out—American Airmen in Stalag Luft 1.* London: Arms and Armour Press.

Many Americans did not join the Eagle Squadrons but remained in the RAF. One of these was Billy Fiske, who was the first American pilot to be killed in the Battle of Britain. His operational details will be found in 601 Squadron's records at the Public Record Office in AIR 27/2068. He is buried at Boxgrove Priory, near Tangmere in Sussex, the fighter station on which he served. There is more about him in Winston G. Ramsey's (ed.) *The Battle of Britain, Then and Now* and in an article by Eunice Wilson in *Nostalgia*, no. 6 (October 1989).

There were others in the Battle, of which these three were the original Eagles of 71 Squadron: Vernon Keough, killed in 1941; Gene Tobin, killed in September 1941; and Andy Mamedoff, killed in October 1941.

Hugh Reilley, buried at Gravesend in the same churchyard as Pocahontas, who also gave her life for freedom in another context, was the second American pilot to be killed in the Battle of Britain in 66 Squadron, whose records are also in AIR 27 at the PRO. Details of all these are found in Haughland (above) and in Ramsey's *The Battle of Britain, Then and Now.*

It is often mistakenly thought that John Gillespie Magee, the pilot poet who wrote "High Flight," was in the Battle. Although he was in Britain at the time, he was still under training, and was killed a year later. See Eunice Wilson's "Poet into Pilot" in *Family Tree Magasine* (June 1989). See also EAGLE SQUADRONS.

Many Americans served in the ATA (Air Transport Auxiliary) and many were women. See WOMEN. For ATA details, see PRO, AVIA class index.

Lettice Curtis's *The Forgotten Pilots* (Olney: Nelson and Saunders, 1971) has useful name lists—male and female, some American. The ATA was an underestimated civilian branch of flying which undertook some courageous duties delivering aircraft in hazardous conditions. Amy Johnson was one of its pilots. The book contains detailed and useful information about a service the RAF was reluctant to accept, but found it could not do without.

Other sources include Combat Reports at PRO, AIR 50/136; Americans at Upavon, Central Flying School PRO, AIR 29/604; list of RAF articles in U.S. magasines listed at the PRO in Flying and Popular Aviation, AIR 2/6327; and Americans in RAF, AIR 2/5163.

ART AND ARTISTS

Books with Portraits of RAF People and War Studies

Ardizzone, Edward. *Diary of a War Artist.* London: Bodley Head, 1974.

Bates, H. E. *War Pictures by British Artists.* No. 3: *RAF.* Oxford: Oxford University Press, 1942.

Helmore, Group Capt W. *Air Commentary.* London: George Allen and Unwin, 1942. Portraits of pilots by Kennington, text by Helmore.

Kennington, Eric. *Drawing the RAF,* Oxford: Oxford University Press, 1942. Portraits.

North, Peter. *Eagles High—50th Anniversary of the Battle of Britain.* London: Leo Cooper, 1990. Evocative drawings and a good glossary.

Taylor, Robert, with Robert Weston. *The Air Combat Paintings of Robert Taylor.* Newton Abbot: David and Charles, 1987. Many other titles and editions of prints by Taylor may be found advertized in air magazines such as *Fly Past.*

Artists and Their Specialities

Clark, Barrie A. F. Aircraft.

Coulson, Gerald. Aircraft.

Emms, Peter. Cover of Beaumont's *My Part of the Sky,* among others.

Hadler, Terry. Cover of Christopher Shore's *Duel for the Sky* (Poole, Dorset: Blandford Press).

Kennington, Eric. One of the most famous of war artists who specialised in RAF portraits.

Knight, Dame Laura. War artist. Examples of work at the Tate Gallery, Imperial War Museum, RAF Museum Hendon and many others. There is a Dame Laura Knight Society. See also the BBC Channel 4 film, September 1989.

Lea, G. E. Painter.

Nockolds, Roy. Paintings of the Battle of Britain. Born 1911, he served with RAF.

Nutkins, Geoffrey. Work exhibited at Shoreham Aviation Museum, Shoreham Village, Sevenoaks, Kent. This area saw the most of the Battle and was nicknamed afterwards "Bomb Alley."

Orde, Cuthbert. Another famous painter of RAF portraits. See cover of Lucas's *Flying Colours*; frontispiece of D. M. Crooke's *Spitfire Pilot* and work in the RAF Museum, Hendon. See also relevant copies of *Illustrated London News,* which may be found at the PRO, or at Colindale Newspaper Library.

Perrott, G. A. Painter.

Snell, Olive. Portraits. Her visits to RAF stations for sittings are mentioned several times in their record books.

Thomas, Christopher. Illustrator and cover artist as well as co-author, with Christopher Shores, of *The Typhoon and Tempest Story* (London: Arms and Armour Press, 1988).

Turner, Michael. Artist of aircraft.

Wootton, Frank. One of the best-known painters of wartime aircraft portraits.

Young, John. Artist of aircraft.

Much of these artists' work is exhibited at the art gallery of the RAF Museum, Hendon.

Galleries

RAF Museum, Hendon, London.

Imperial War Museum, Lambeth, London.

Tangmere Military Museum.

Aeroart (FP), 2 Higher Downs, Knutsford Rd., Cheshire WA16 6AW.

Aviation Art International, 88 Durwin Rd., Bridlington, Yorks YO16 5HZ.

Buccaneer Distribution Ltd., Unit 4, Linwood Workshops, Linwood Lane, Leicestershire LE2 6QJ.

Callow, 104 Kirkham Street, Plumstead, London SE16 2EN.

Collectair Limited Editions, 6 Hanover Rd., Norwich, NR2 2HD.

The advertising pages of magasines such as *Fly Past, The Air War* and *RAF News* list galleries and painters as sources from where prints may be obtained by mail order.

There is also the annual exhibition of The Guild of Aviation Artists, Unit 5016a, Bondway Bus Centre 71, Bondway, London SW8, from where details may be obtained.

ASSOCIATIONS AND SOCIETIES

Air Britain, International Association of Aviation Historians, 1 East Street, Tonbridge, Kent.

Aircrew Association, 19 Marescroft Rd., Britwell Estate, Slough, Bucks.

American Aviation Historical Society, Washington, D.C.

Arnold Register, 51 Henley Rd., Leicester LE3 9RD. Although this was formed in 1942 to bring together those who trained in America under the Arnold and the Powers Schemes, it is useful for name tracing, though it does not specifically list those of the Battle of Britain.

Battle of Britain Fighter Association, 71 The Brow, Widley, Portsmouth PO7 5BY.

Blenheim Society, 5 Oaks, 13 Wellington Rd., Enfield, Mdx, England EN 1 2 PD.

Catalina Society, Plane Sailing Air Displays, 24 Batts Hill, Reigate, Surrey RH2 OLT.

Caterpillar Club, c/o Irvin GB Ltd., Ickneild Way, Letchworth, Herts S96 IEV.

Cross and Cockade. Cragg Cottage, The Craggs, Bramham, Wetherby West Yorkshire. WW1 but has references to WW2.

Friends of RAF Museum, c/o Hendon Museum, London NW9.

Goldfish Club, RAF Reserve Club, 14 South St., London W1. The Club was founded by Charles A. Robertson, chief of Aircraft Production, Air Sea Rescue Equipment.

Guinea Pig Club. See Edward Bishop, *The Guinea Pig Club* (London: Macmillan, 1963), on the treatment of burned aircrew.

Odd Bods, UK Association, P.O. Box 166, Kincumber 2250 NSW Australia.

Polish Air Force Association, 14 Collingham Gardens, London SW5.

RAF Benevolent Fund, 67 Portland Place, London W1 4AR. See Edward Bishop's *The Debt We Owe: RAF Benevolent Fund 1919—1969* (London: Longmans, 1969).

RAF Escaping Society (the Dodgers), 206 Brompton Road, London SW. Formed 1945 to bring together those who helped British and American airmen in France during the German occupation. See A. J. Evans' *The Escapers' Club* (London: Bodley Head) (stories by the Club members). See also description in Denis Richards' *Portal of Hungerford* (London: Heinemann, 1977).

Royal Aeronautical Society, 4 Hamilton Place, London W1.

Royal Air Force Association (RAFA), 43 Grove Park Road, Chiswick, London W4 3RV. Has regional and local branches, incorporating all ranks.

Royal Air Force Historical Society, c/o Royal Aeronautical Society, or Membership Secretary, 28 Shirley Drive, Worthing, West Sussex.

Royal Netherlands Air Force Recovery Unit (15 men under the command of Major Ane de Jong recovered Allied aircraft from the Zuider Zee). Contact RNAF.

Spitfire Society, Hall of Aviation, Albert Rd. South, Southampton SO1 IFR.

Warbirds Worldwide, Mansfield, Nots NG20 8BN.

Squadron associations are listed in the acknowledgments pages of Richard Collier's *Eagle Day*. But many more have been formed since, for example, 501 Squadron Association, c/o Bristol University Air Squadron, and 247 (F) China British Squadron Association, 143 Harbord Street, London SW6 6PN. Other associations and reunions are advertised in *RAF News, Fly Past* and *Air Mail.*

AUSTRALIANS

Air Battle Europe 1935–45. Australians at War series. Battle of Britain to D Day.

Bevis, Lewis S., ed. *Odd Bods at War 1939–45: Aussies in the RAF*. Kinkumber, New South Wales: 1990.

AWARDS, MEDALS AND DECORATIONS

Listings of the Distinguished Flying Cross and Medal, the Air Force Cross and Medal, Distinguished Service Order and others, including promotions, are in the *London Gazette* under these headings. They can be found in the quarterly indices under the recipient's name, but if the date is not known a long search will be required. Sometimes, but not always, the full citation is given for all ranks. Earlier awards are listed under State Intelligence in the *London Gazette*, PRO ref ZJ1. From January 1942 onward this was altered and the names appear alphabetically under Honours, Decorations and Medals. If the actual recommendation to the Sovereign is required, look in PRO AIR 30 for several weeks before the date awarded, and also in the squadron's operations books, AIR 27. (For example, see 1940: AIR 30/157 for several names.) Miscellaneous other related documents may also be found here. Awards, however, have been found to be wrongly indexed or omitted altogether, so cross check wherever possible.

Reports of awards and decorations will be noted in a squadron's operational record book, and in AIR 2/30 and AIR 30/157 for 1940 at the PRO, but the date must be known. These are also reported in the *London Gazette*, the index of which (quarterly) will give the page reference. It is necessary to look several weeks following the award in the *London Gazette* to allow for printing and publication. See also the following:

Abbott, P. E., and Tamplin, J.M.A. *British Gallantry Awards*. London: Guinness Superlatives, 1971. Lists some names; describes and illustrates the decoration and quotes examples. Good bibliography.

Dorling, H. Tapprell. *Ribbons and Medals*. London: Phillips, 1974. Good index, bibliography and colour illustrations. This author is the writer Taffrail.

Several magasines and journals are devoted to medals and their research. There is a Medal Roll on microfiche at the PRO for WW1 but not for WW2.

The DFC was awarded for flying on active operations; the AFC for non-operational flying; and the MC for ground operations. All these were awarded to officers, including junior and Warrant Officers.

The equivalent for Warrant Officers, NCOs and other ranks were the DFM, for operational flying; the AFM, for non-operational flying; the DCM, for ground operations; and the GCM, for flying on active service. See PRO leaflet 108 and the Air Historical Branch, MoD. Details of awards may be obtained by next of kin from MoD, RAF Innsworth, Personnel Management Centre, Gloucester GL3 1E2.

The sales catalogues of auction houses offer several useful clues for the following up of medals awarded and then sold. Although there are several medal specialists, Sotheby's, Christie's and Bonhams' are the main specialists offering military memorabilia regularly. For example, see: Sotheby's, London (Catalogue for sale, 10 November 1988, referred to as ''Scramble.'' RAF list from page 59: among the items are listed the medals of Group Captain Peter Townsend, CO of 85 Squadron, Battle of Britain, CVO, DSO, DFC. With quotes from *London Gazette*. Illustration by Capt. Cuthbert Orde and many photographs. Sold with his log books. Reference to book titles.).

Other auction houses hold sales of militaria and issue similar catalogues. It is worth obtaining past and present issues.

BATTLE OF BRITAIN, MISCELLANEOUS WORKS ABOUT

Air Ministry. *The Battle of Britain*. London: Department for Air Training, Pamphlet 156, August 1943.

Air Ministry Public Relations. *A Short History of the Battle of Britain*. London: 1960.

Anthony, Gordon, and John MacAdam. *Air Aces*. London: Home and Van Thal, 1944.

Armitage, Sqn Ldr Dennis. "The Battle of Britain." *The Elevator* (journal of the Lancashire Aero Club) (Spring/Autumn 1958).

Atkins, Peter. *Buffoon in Flight*. Johannesburg: Ernest Stanton, 1979. 24 Sqn.

Barker, Ralph. *Down in the Drink*. London: Chatto and Windus, 1955. True stories of the Goldfish Club.

Battle of Britain Gift Book. Purnell, London: 1969. From the "great new motion picture."

Bickers, R. T. *Ginger Lacey, Fighter Pilot*. London: Robert Hale, 1962. Battle of Britain ace.

Birkby, Carel. *Dancing in the Skies*. Capetown: Howard Timmins, 1982.

Brittain, Vera. *England's Hour*. London: Macmillan, 1941.

Burn, Michael. *Mary and Richard*. London: Andre Deutsch, 1988.

Carne, Daphne. *The Eyes of the Few*. London: Macmillan, 1960.

Cockerell, Geoffrey. "Remembering the Few." 40th Anniversary Review. A supplement by the news editor of the *Southampton Evening News*, 1990.

Collier, Basil. *The Defence of the United Kingdom*. London: HMSO, 1957.

———. *The Leader of the Few*. London: Jarrolds, 1957. Authorised biography of Lord Dowding.

Czernin, Count Manfred, with Norman L. R. Franks. *Double Mission*. London: William Kimber, 1976. About Count Manfred Czernin, RAF Fighter Ace and SOE Agent.

Finnie, G. K. "Lessons of the Battle of Britain." *Roundel* 1, no. 6.

Foreman, John. *The Battle of Britain—The Forgotten Months, November-December 1940*. New Malden, Surrey: Air Research, 1988. Very well documented by date, with daily list of casualties of both sides.

Foster, Reginald. *Dover Front*. London: Secker and Warburg, 1941.

Graves, Charles. *The Thin Blue Line*. London: Hutchinson, 1941.

Gribble, Leonard R. *Epics of the Fighting RAF*. London: Harrap, 1943.

Hall, Roger. *Clouds of Fear*. Reprint, 1975. Folkestone: Bailey, 1970.

Haslam, Gp Capt E. B. "How Lord Dowding Came to Leave Fighter Command." *Journal of Strategic Studies* (June 1981).

Hill, Air Marshal Sir Roderick. "The Fighters' Greatest Day." *Journal of the Royal Air Force* 3, no. 5.

Johnstone, Air Vice Marshal Sandy. *Enemy in the Sky*. London: William Kimber, 1976. 1940 London.

Parkinson, Roger. *Dawn on Our Darkness*. London: Granada, 1977. The summer of 1940.

Port of London Association Monthly. "Air Defences of the Port of London." May 1945.

Ramsey, Winston G., ed. *The Battle of Britain, Then and Now*. London: After the Battle Publications, 1980. Revised regularly. The bible of the Battle of Britain researcher.

Sims, E. *The Fighter Pilots*. London: Cassell, 1967. Monographs of the Aces.

———. *Fighter Tactics 1914–70*. London: Cassell, 1972. Shows little change between tactics of the two wars, except that the freelance fighter had gone and was now one of a team.

Tolliver, R. *The Blond Knight of Germany*. London: Barker, 1970. Describes A. Hartman.

Townsend, Peter. *Duel of Eagles*. London: Weidenfeld and Nicholson, 1970.

———. *Time and Chance*. London: Collins, 1978. See also his *Duel in the Dark*.

The Untold Story of the Battle of Britain. New Malden, Surrey: Air Research Publications, 1988. Bomber, Coastal and Training Command.

Winchester, Barry. *Eighty Four Days—The Battle of Britain Remembered*. London: Selma, 1974. A rhyming appreciation of the Battle of Britain.

Winter, D. *The First of the Few*. London: Allen Lane, 1982. Ordinary fighter pilots of WW1 from enlistment to demob, many of whom went on to be the staff officers of the Battle of Britain.

Wood, Derek. *Target England*. London: Janes, 1980. Illustrated history of the Battle of Britain. See also Wood and D. Dempster, *The Narrow Margin*, 1961.

Wright, R. C. *Dowding and the Battle of Britain*. London: Macdonald, 1967.

———. *Spitfire and Hurricane Tribute*. Booklet. Battle of Britain Memorial Flight. RAF Coningsby.

BATTLE OF BRITAIN, WORKS SPECIFICALLY ABOUT

Bailey, Jim. *The Sky Suspended*. London: Hodder and Stoughton, 1965.

Barker, Ralph. *That Eternal Summer, Unknown Stories from the Battle of Britain*. London: Collins, 1990.

Bartley, Sqn Ldr Anthony, DFC. *Smoke Trails in the Sky: 92 Squadron*. London: William Kimber 1956. Author saw action in 92 Sqn with Stanford Tuck.

Bartz, Karl. *Swastika in the Sky*. London: William Kimber, 1956.

Braham, Wg Cdr J.R.D. *Scramble*. London: William Kimber, 1961.

Burt, Kendal, and James Leasor. *The One That Got Away*. New York: Random Press, 1957; London: Collins, 1956. About the German Luftwaffe Ace Franz von Werra. See also P. R. Reid, MBE MC, *My Favourite Escape Stories* (London: Lutterworth Press, 1975).

Churchill, Winston. *Their Finest Hour*. Boston: Houghton Mifflin, 1949. Do not confuse with *Finest Hour* by Martin Gilbert (London: Heinemann, 1989). See also Churchill's *Great War Speeches* (London: Corgi, 1978.)

Clout, Charles. *Swastika over Sussex*. Tonbridge, Kent: Air Britain, 1956.

Fleming, Peter. *Operation Sea Lion*. New York: Simon and Schuster, 1963.

Gelb, Norman. *Scramble!* London: Michael Joseph, 1986. A narrative history of the Battle of Britain.

Gibbs, AVM Gerald. *Survivor's Story*. London: Hutchinson, 1956. Autobiography of a WW1 fighter pilot who served in 11 Group HQ in the Battle of Britain.

Gilbert, Martin. *Finest Hour: Winston Churchill, 1939–1941*. London: Heinemann, 1983. Good index and footnotes.

Jullian, Marcel. *The Battle of Britain*. London: Jonathan Cape, 1956; Bath: Cedric Chivers, 1974. Translated from the French. Good bibliography, which includes French and German titles, and squadrons by number. There is also an account of von Werra's interrogation in "The Cage." Cross reference this with Burt and Leasor's *The One That Got Away*. "The Cage" was the house in which all PoWs were questioned. It still stands in "Millionaires' Row," behind the gates of Palace Green, Kensington. This is a private road.

Kent, J. A. *One of the Few*. London: William Kimber, 1971. The author led a fighter squadron in the Battle.

Lewis, J. H. "London Diary." *Air Britain Digest* 4, no. 5 (1953).

McKee, Alexander. *Strike from the Sky*. London: Souvenir Press, 1960.

Mee, Arthur. *1940*. London: Hodder and Stoughton, 1941. The series The Kings England, by county, gives historical background to many places mentioned in RAF accounts.

Meteorological Office, Bracknell. Weather in the Battle of Britain.

Middleton, Drew. *The Sky Suspended*. London: Secker and Warburg, 1960. Battle of Britain and the Blitz.

Reid, John M. *Some of the Few*. London: Macdonald, 1960.

Simpson, Gp Capt William. *One of Our Pilots Is Safe*. London: Hamish Hamilton, 1942. Author was in East Grinstead Hospital as a Guinea Pig with Richard Hillary.

The *Annual Register 1940*, Vol. 182, gives details of this period, which was not yet designated as the Battle of Britain. This can be found complete on the open shelves at the PRO and in most central reference libraries.

BATTLE OF BRITAIN HQs

Fighter Command Headquarters was at Bentley Priory, a house with a long history before the RAF took it over. That of Bomber Command was at High Wycombe. Both are still in existence and operational, though they have other functions today. Other Commands and Group Commands are often equally in places of long and historical tradition. To gain an overall picture, one should study the local terrain. The Command HQs are not open to visitors, though large houses once used by them in the area may be.

For background history of the original site, see the following:

Coppock, J. T., and Hugh C. Price, eds. *Greater London*. London: Faber and Faber, 1964.

Fitzgerald, Percy. *Victoria's London*. London: Alderman Press, 1984.

Harley, J. B. *Historian's Guide to Survey Maps*. London: National Council of Social Services, 1965.

The Village London Atlas: The Changing Face of Greater London, 1822–1903. London: Alderman Press, 1986. (Other original Victorian sites on which Battle of Britain RAF Stations and HQs were built may be studied in this book, for example, North Weald, Uxbridge, Hendon, and Chigwell.)

Its RAF story will be found at the PRO in AIR 16/408.

For Uxbridge, Stanmore, High Wycombe, and Northolt, see AIR 28 at the PRO, in the ORBs of Squadrons AIR 27, and in AIR 29 under unit description or AIR 16 Fighter Command. See also AIRFIELDS section in this volume.

Ordnance Survey maps may be obtained at any good map shop and in good reference libraries. The Ordnance Survey HQ is at Romsey Rd., Southampton, and in London at Hampton House, 20 Albert Embankment, SE 1.

"BATTLE OF BRITAIN" IN THE TITLE, WORKS WITH

Allen, Wg Cdr Hubert Raymond "Dizzy," DFC. *The Battle for Britain.* London: Arthur Barker, 1973; London: Corgi, 1973.

———. *Who Won The Battle of Britain?* London: Arthur Barker, 1974; London: Panther, 1976. Controversial criticism by a Battle pilot. Good bibliography.

Armitage, Sqn Ldr Dennis. "The Battle of Britain." *The Elevator* (journal of the Lancashire Aero Club) (Spring/Autumn 1958).

"The Battle of Britain." In *Great Campaigns of World War II,* J. B. Davies. London: Phoebus Publishing, 1980; Macdonald, 1988.

"The Battle of Britain." Icare, *Revue de Pilotes de Ligne.* No. 35–36 (Autumn/Winter 1965). English and French text.

Battle of Britain Memorial Flight, brochure. Lincolnshire: RAF Coningsby. Not for resale.

Battle of Britain Museum. Various guides booklets. RAF Museum, Hendon, London.

Battle of Britain Museum. Booklets. Hawkinge, Kent.

Bishop, Edward. *The Battle of Britain.* London: Allen and Unwin, 1960.

Boorman, H.R.P., and H. R. Long. *Recalling the Battle of Britain.* Maidstone: Kent Messenger, 1965.

Clark, Ronald W. *The Battle for Britain.* London: George Harrap, 1975. Sixteen weeks that changed the course of history.

Collier, Basil. *The Battle of Britain.* London: Batsford, 1962.

———. *The Battle of Britain.* London: Jackdaw Publications, Jonathan Cape, 1969. Jackdaw 65; includes folder with 20 inserts, facsimiles, etc., for study.

Collyer, David G. *Battle of Britain, Diary of Events—East Kent.* Maidstone: Kent Defence Research Group, Kent Aviation Historical Society, 1980. Kent was the county most directly involved, as it was in the line of takeoff from Germany. Later it was called "Bomb Alley."

Cooksley, Peter G. *The Battle of Britain.* London: Ian Allan, 1990.

Cooksley, Peter G., and Richard Ward. *The Battle of Britain—Hurricane, Spitfire, Messerschmitt Bf 109.* London: Osprey, 1968.

Davies, Walford. *Battle of Britain.* Film music and march, recorded by EMI.

Deighton, Len. *The Battle of Britain.* London: Jonathan Cape, 1980.

Dowding, Air Chief Marshal Sir Hugh C. T. "The Battle of Britain." Supplement to the *London Gazette,* 11 September 1946. In MoD Adastral Library. 20 August 1941.

Fox, Edward. *The Battle of Britain.* London: Lutterworth Press, 1969. Illustrated by Will Nickless.

Frankland, N., and E. Dowling, eds. "The Battle of Britain." In *The Decisive Battles of the Twentieth Century.* London: Sidgwick and Jackson, 1976.

Franks, Norman. *The Battle of Britain.* London: Bison Books, 1981. Good maps of stations.

Gibbs, Air Vice Marshal Gerald. "The Battle of Britain." *Journal of the United Services Institute of India* 83, pp. 352–53.

HMSO. *The Battle of Britain, 1940.* London: HMSO, 1941.

———. *The Battle of Britain: An Account of the Great Days from 8 August to 31 October 1940.* London: Air Ministry, 1941. Written anonymously by Air Ministry. Reprinted in facsimile, 1989.

Hobbs, Anthony. *The Battle of Britain*. Hove, Sussex: Wayland, 1973.

Hough, Richard. *The Battle of Britain*. New York: Macmillan, 1971.

Hutchinson, Tom. *The Battle of Britain*. London: Purnell, 1960. Illustrated from film of the same name.

Johnson, J. E. "Johnnie," Air Vice Marshal, with Wg Cdr P. B. "Laddie" Lucas. *Glorious Summer: The Story of the Battle of Britain*. London: Stanley Paul, 1990.

Julian, Marcel. *The Battle of Britain*, New York: Orion Press, 1965; London: Cedric Chivers and Jonathan Cape, 1967, 1974. Translated from the French. A former pilot bases his account on interviews with those who were there on both sides of the Channel.

Kent, Gp Capt John. "The Battle of Britain." *Polish Airman's Weekly Review* (June 1957). Extracts from the personal diary of the English commander of a Polish squadron.

Lecerf, J. L. "La Bataille Aerienne d'Angleterre." *Forces Aerienne Française*, 10 Année, no. 107.

Department of Member for Air Training, Air Ministry. *The Battle of Britain*, AMP 156. 1943. The Battle of Britain.

Mason, Frank. *Battle over Britain*. London: McWhirter Twins, 1960, 1969; updated, London: Aston, 1990. History of German assaults on Britain, 1917–18, and July–December 1940.

Ministry of Defence Directorate of Public Relations (RAF). *The Battle of Britain*. 25th Anniversary, 1965.

Moseley, Leonard. *The Battle of Britain*. London: Pan, 1969. The making of the film.

Moseley, Leonard, et al. *The Battle of Britain*. London: Time-Life Books, 1977.

Munston, Ken, and John W. R. Taylor. *The Battle of Britain*. London: New English Library, 1976.

North, Peter. *Eagles High: The Battle of Britain 50th Anniversary*. London: Leo Cooper, 1990. Drawings and good glossary.

Price, Alfred. *The Hardest Day: The Battle of Britain*. London: Jane's, 1979.

Ramsey, Winston G., ed. *The Battle of Britain, Then and Now*. London: After the Battle Publications, 1980. Several revised versions. This is the Battle of Britain researcher's "bible." Deeply researched via name, date and squadron, it is the most comprehensive book on the subject and where all research should begin after the preliminary readings as initially outlined.

Reid, John M. *The Battle of Britain*. London: HMSO, 1960.

———. *The Battle of Britain: a Short History* (commemorating the 20th Anniversary). London: Air Ministry, 1960.

Richards, Dennis. "The Battle of Britain." In *The History of the Second World War*, Vol. 1, No. 12. London: Purnell, 1966.

Robertson, Bruce. *The Battle of Britain*. Sun Valley, Calif.: Air Historians Model Books, 1976.

———. *Spitfire: The Story of the Famous Fighter*. London: Harleyford Press, 1960.

Saunders, Hillary St George. *The Battle of Britain*. London: Tandem, 1969. Contains the Air Ministry account previously mentioned, written anonymously by Saunders from official contemporary documents. Other contributors include Richard Hillary and Cajus Bekker.

Smith, N. D. *The Battle of Britain*. Men and Events series. London: Faber and Faber,

1962. Twelve months from May 1940 to May 1941. Quotes from pilots and civilians.

Spaight, J. M. *The Battle of Britain, 1940*. London: Geoffrey Bles, 1941.

Townsend, Peter. "La Bataille d'Angleterre." *Forces Aerienne Française*, no. 61–65 (August–September 1955); *Paris Match*, 17 September and 24 September 1966.

Walton, William. *The Battle of Britain Suite*. Music for film by United Artists, 1969.

Winslade, Richard. *The Battle of Britain Memorial Flight*. London: Osprey, updated periodically.

Wynn, Kenneth G. *Men of The Battle of Britain*. Norwich: Gliddon Books, 1989. Who's who of the pilots and aircrew—British, Commonwealth, and Allied—who flew with Fighter Command, 10 July to 31 October 1940. With a foreword by Her Majesty the Queen Mother, patron of the Battle of Britain Fighter Association. The main reference source of biography and service detail. The acknowledgments and bibliography will prove useful to the researcher.

THE BATTLE ON THE GROUND

Barker, Felix. "Twenty Four Hours that Saved Britain." *London Evening News*, September 12–17, 1940.

Boorman, H. R. P. *Hell's Corner, 1940*. Maidstone: Kent Messenger, 1940.

Bowen, Elizabeth. *The Heat of the Day*. London, 1949. A novel about the Blitz.

Clayton, Aileen. *The Enemy Is Listening*. New York: Ballantine, 1960; London: Hutchinson, 1980. The story of the Y service.

Collier, Basil. *The City that Wouldn't Die*. New York: E. P. Dutton, 1960.

Downes, Mollie Panter. *London War Notes: Letter from England, 1940*. Boston, MA: Atlantic Monthly Press, 1940–end of war. Author was London correspondent of the *New Yorker*.

Foster, Reginald. *Dover Front*. London: Secker and Warburg, 1941.

Folkestone, Hythe, and District Herald. "Front Line Folkestone." 1945.

Grant, Ian, and Nicholas Madden. *The City at War*. London: Jupiter, 1975.

———. *The Countryside at War*. London: Jupiter, 1975.

———. London Transport at War series.

Graves, Charles. *The Home Guard of Britain*. London: Hutchinson.

HMSO. *The Defence of the United Kingdom*. London: HMSO, 1957.

———. *London: Front Line 1940–41*. London: HMSO, 1942.

Illingworth, F. *Britain under Shellfire*. London: Hutchinson, 1942.

Kee, Robert, and Joanna Smith. *We'll Meet Again*. London: Dent, 1984. The title is taken from one of the most popular of wartime songs, sung by Vera Lynn, the Forces Sweetheart. Other songs by her are still obtainable on disc or tape.

Knight, G. "Five Hundred Hours in the Blitz." British Library, Typescripts MS.

Leslie, Anita. *A Story Half Told*. London: Hutchinson, 1983. Autobiographical experiences in wartime London.

Lewey, F. R. *Cockney Campaign*. London: Stanley Paul, 1947.

———. *The Real Dad's Army: Story of the Home Guard*. London: Hutchinson, 1974.

Lewis, J. H. "London Diary." *Air Britain Digest* 4, no. 5 (1953).

Lewis, Peter. *A People's War*. London: Thames/Methuen, 1986. Channel Four Book. Good bibliography.

Longmate, Norman. *If Britain Had Fallen.* London: BBC/Hutchinson, 1974.
Mack, Joanna, and Steve Humphries. *London at War: The Making of Modern London, 1939–45.* London: Sidgwick and Jackson, 1985. Well illustrated, with good further reading list. Recommends INFRA/264 on, at PRO, and Intelligence on Morale and Mass Observation Archive at University of Sussex.
Marchant, Hilda. *Women and Children Last.* London: Victor Gollancz, 1941. A woman reporter's view of the Battle of Britain.
Matthews, Very Rev. W. R. *St Paul's Cathedral in Wartime.* London: Hutchinson. The City's cathedral, against the flames, is the central feature that symbolises both the Battle and the Blitz.
Mee, Arthur. *1940.* London: Hodder and Stoughton, 1941.
Meteorological Office. *The Weather in the Battle of Britain.* HMSO, Bracknell.
Milburn, Clara. *Mrs Milburn's Diaries.* Ed. Peter Donnelly. London: Harrap, 1979. An Englishwoman's day to day reflections, 1939–45. One-sided and biased, of course, with an inability to read between the lines of her POW son's letters, nevertheless a factual account, particularly of the bombing in the Midlands.
Murrow, Edward R. *This Is London.* London: Cassell, 1941.
Nancarrow, Fred E. "The Defence of the Teleprinter Network." *Post Office Electrical Engineers* 38, pt. 4 (London).
"Night Shift." *Journal of the Royal Artillery* 75 no. 11. Work of the AA Searchlights.
O'Brien, T. H. *Civil Defence.* London: HMSO and Longmans, Green, 1955.
Park, Air Chief Marshal Sir Keith. "Background to the Blitz." *Hawker Siddeley Review* (December 1951).
Pile, General Sir Frederick. *Ack Ack.* London: Harrap, 1949.
Ramsey, L. F. "West Wittering in the Front Line." *Sussex County Magasine* (Eastbourne).
Randle-Ford, J. M. *A Dorset Village's War Effort.* Bournemouth: Roman Press, 1945.
Robins, Gordon. *Fleet Street Blitz Diary.* London: Ernest Benn, 1944.
Storrer, J. D. *Behind the Scenes in an Aircraft Factory.* 1965.
Thompson, Lawrence. *1940: Year of Legend, Year of History.* London: Collins, 1966.
Wallington, Neil. *Fireman!* London: David and Charles, 1979.
———. *Fireman at War.* London: David and Charles, 1981.

Home Office Records at the PRO may give more information; see HO indexes:

HO 186	Air Raid Precautions
HO 192	Air Raid Damage
HO 208	ARP and Home Security Circular
HO 220	Ministry of Home Security Supplement

The following abbreviations are used in most governmental material. There could be further information in these PRO (Kew) files, which are other than the usual AIR files in which Battle of Britain background may be located. Research in this area will depend on how much is needed on the support given to the RAF by those on the ground, and how they withstood the Battle.

MAP: Ministry of Aircraft Production

MAF: Ministry of Agriculture and Fisheries (Food)

Local parish registers for 1940 are available at the church, in the local history library, or the County Record Office.

BIBLIOGRAPHIES AND DATABASES

Adastral Library, Ministry of Defence. *Bibliography of the Royal Air Force*. Scotland Yard, London: Adastral Library of the Ministry of Defence. In four parts: 1, The Force; 2, The Operations; 3, The Personalties; 4, The Aircraft. This work is based on the stock of the Ministry of Defence at the Adastral Library (Air) and dates back to the birth of the Service. There are no classified titles included, and the Library is being constantly updated. Most have been commercially available. The Library is open by appointment to bona fide researchers stating their requirements.

BLAISE-LINE. This is an on-line bibliographic service run by the British Library. It is computer based and is composed of over 8 million records, which cover British books on all subjects since 1950, including forthcoming titles; *the British Library Catalogue*, covering material on all subjects acquired in two centuries; *the Humanities and Social Science Catalogue*, which has material in all major languages; *Worldwide Publications—Library of Congress Database*; catalogue of University of London; Scientific and Business Publications; Government Publications; Material originating in Europe; Audiovisual material; the Map Library. BNBMARC and LCMARC files cover virtually all the world's books. Enquiries should be made to BL Bibliographic Services, 2 Sheraton St., London WIV 4BH, tel 01-636 1544.

HMSO. *List of Current Papers* (1965) 016.62913 for the Aeronautical Research Council. Updated frequently.

Richards, Denis. *Portal of Hungerford*. London: Heinemann, 1977. Does not contain a bibliography as such, but the list of references per chapter for PRO material for the year 1940 make locating them simple.

Terraine, John. *The Right of the Line: The RAF in European War, 1939–45*. London: Hodder and Stoughton, 1985. This is a book no researcher of this period should be without. It is more than a valuable contribution by an eminent historian; it is the background detail from which all other Air Force research should begin. The bibliography is comprehensive.

Warren Springs Lab. 1958–64. "The human factor in the design of cockpits." Aircraft construction. 016.629134.

Wells, A. J., gen. ed. *The British National Bibliography*. Annual volumes available in most main district libraries. Council of British National Bibliography Ltd., British Museum.

Many other books on the RAF and the Battle of Britain include detailed specialist bibliographies. These are mentioned in this volume, but should be consulted before going to the British Library or BLAISE-LINE, as readers' tickets are required for the former.

BIOGRAPHIES AND PERSONALITIES

Anthony, Gordon, and John Macadam. *Air Aces.* London: Home and Van Thal, 1944.

Barrymaine, Norman. *The Story of Peter Townsend.* London: Peter Davies, 1958.

Barthropp, Wg Cdr Patrick. *Paddy: The Life and Times of Wg Cdr Paddy Barthropp.* London: Baker, 1987. See also "The Gallant Few," *Daily Telegraph* colour supplement, September 1988.

Beamont, Wg Cdr Roland. *Fighter Test Pilot.* Wellingborough: Patrick Stephens, 1985. About Beamont see also *Against the Sun* by Edward Lanchberry (London: Cassell, 1955).

———. *My Part of the Sky.* Wellingborough: Patrick Stephens, 1989.

———. *Phoenix into Ashes.* London: William Kimber, 1968. First British pilot to fly at speed of sound. A Battle of Britain pilot, DSO OBE DFC.

Bennett, Air Vice Marshal D.C.T. *Pathfinder.* London: Muller, 1958. His own story. See also Alan Bramson, *Master Airman,* below.

Bickers, Richard Townshend. *Ginger Lacey, Fighter Pilot.* London: Robert Hale, 1962; Pan Books, Battle of Britain series, 1969.

Bolitho, Hector. *Penguin in the Eyrie.* London: Hutchinson, 1955. RAF diary of an Intelligence Officer, 1939-45.

Boyle, Andrew. *Trenchard: Man of Vision.* London: Collins, 1962. "Father" of the RAF.

Bramson, Alan. *Master Airman.* Shrewsbury: Air Life, 1985. About AVM Donald Bennett. There are several other books by this author about flying in general. An examiner instructor.

Brickhill, Paul. *Reach for the Sky.* London: Collins, 1954. The story of Douglas Bader, one of the greatest heroes of the Battle. There are other books about and by him.

Burn, Michael. *Mary and Richard.* London: Andre Deutsch, 1988. Personal letters from and to Richard Hillary, the most well-known and tragic figure of the Battle of Britain. Written by Mary's husband. See Hillary's *The Last Enemy,* his own account of the disfiguring burns which changed his life. See also the biography by Lovat Dickson, below.

Clostermann, Pierre. *The Big Show.* London: Chatto and Windus, 1951; London: Corgi, 1965. French fighter pilot in the RAF. Translated from the French by Oliver Berthond.

———. *Flames in the Sky.* London: Chatto and Windus, 1952; Beaver Books, 1960.

———. *War in the Air, 1940–45.* London: Corgi, 1966.

Darlington, Roger. *Night Hawk.* London: William Kimber, 1985. About the Czech ace Karel Kuttelwascher, by his son-in-law. Good bibliography in English and Czech. Well illustrated. See also *The Saturday Book* (1944) and an article in *The People.*

Deere, Alan. *Nine Lives.* London: Hodder and Stoughton, 1959.

Dickson, Lovat. *Richard Hillary.* London: Macmillan, 1950. See Michael Burn, above. Had he lived Hillary would have been a great writer.

Douglas, Sholto, Marshal of the Royal Air Force. *The Years of Combat.* Vol. 1 of autobiography. *Second World War,* Vol. 2 (with Robert Wright). London: Collins, 1966.

Dundas, Sir Hugh. *Flying Start: A Fighter Pilot's War Years*. London: Stanley Paul, 1988.

Furniss-Roe, Bill. *Believed Safe*. London: William Kimber, 1987. A fighter pilot's double escape. 66 Sqn.

Gleave, T. P. *I Had a Row with a German*. London: Macmillan, 1941.

Gleed, Wg Cdr Ian, DSO, DFC. *Arise to Conquer*. London: Gollancz, 1942.

Kelly, Terence. *Hurricane and Spitfire Pilots at War*. London: William Kimber, 1986.

Kent, J. A. *One of the Few*. London: William Kimber, 1971.

Mitchell, Gordon. *R. J. Mitchell, World Famous Aircraft Designer*. Nelson and Saunders, 1990.

Norris, G. "McKellar: Scottish Ace." *RAF Flying Review* 15, no. 6.

Offenberg, Jean. *Lonely Warrior*. London: Souvenir Press, 1956; New York: Taplinger, 1956; Granada: Mayflower, 1969. Belgian Fighter pilot with 145 and 609 Squadron. Edited from his diaries. Photos of his funeral are in H. Frank Ziegler, *Under the White Rose*.

Orange, Vincent. *The Road to Biggin Hill*. Shrewsbury: AirLife. About Johnny Checketts, NZ.

———. *Sir Keith Park*. London: Methuen, 1984. Good chapter notes, bibliography and PRO references.

Orde, Cuthbert. *Pilots of Fighter Command*. London: Harrap, 1942. Drawings.

Page, Geoffrey. *Tale of a Guinea Pig*. London: Pelham Books, 1981. Badly burnt pilot with DSO, DFC, who survived.

Pelican History of the World. "Battle of Britain." Chapter covers the official dates of 10 July to 31 October. Contains quotes from Jeffrey Quill's *Spitfire* (John Murray): "In scale, the Battle of Britain was small by comparison with the air ops which took place later, but its effects were enormous."

Penrose, Harold. *Architect of Wings*. Shrewsbury: Air Life, 1985. Biography of Roy Chadwick, designer of the Lancaster. Not about the Battle of Britain, but includes 1940.

Philpott, Bryan. *Famous Fighter Aces*. Thorsons, Wellingborough: Patrick Stephens, 1989. Good bibliography, lists aces of WW1 and 2, RAF, RCAF, USAAF and Luftwaffe.

Richards, Denis. *Portal of Hungerford*. London: Heinemann, 1977. Good bibliography and PRO reference.

Richardson, Anthony. *Wingless Victory*. London: Odhams, 1950. See also Basil Embry, *Mission Completed*.

Richie, Wg Cdr Paul. *Fighter Pilot*. London: Batsford, 1941. First published anonymously, reissued 1955. Revised, London: Pan Books, 1969, to include maps and diagrams. See also Frank H. Ziegler's *Under the White Rose*, story of 609 Sqn, whose CO Michael Robinson was Richie's brother-in-law.

Saward, Gp Capt Dudley. *Bomber Harris*. London: Buchan and Enright, 1985. The authorised biography. See also the TV film, September 1989.

Sharp, Martin, ed. *Diary of Sir Geoffrey de Havilland*. Author is editor of *Air Transport*.

Steinhilper, Ulrich. *Spitfire on My Tail*. Keston, Kent: Independent Books, 1989. German pilot of the Battle of Britain, flew with 3/JG52 from Pas de Calais.

Stevenson, Sqn Ldr D. L. *Five Crashes Later*. London: William Kimber. Hurricane and Tempest pilot.

Stokes, Douglas. *Paddy Finucane*. London: William Kimber, 1983. The story of the Irish fighter ace who became a flight commander with the first Australian squadron in Britain, 452. Died in 1942 with 32 enemy aircraft to his credit. Very good research notes and combat summaries.

———. *Wings Aflame*. London: William Kimber, 1984. Biography of Gp Capt Beamish DSO/bar DFC, AFC. Flew 126 fighter sorties after solo in a Hurricane. Station Commander in Battle of Britain.

Sutton, Gp Capt Barry. *The Way of a Pilot*. London: Macmillan, 1942.

———. *The Summer of the Firebrand.* Poetry of the Battle of Britain.

Taylor, A.J.P. Lord Beaverbrook, a Biography. Minister of Aircraft Production and father of Wg Cdr Max Aitken, 98 Squadron.

Tedder, Lord Arthur William, Marshal of the Royal Air Force. *War Memories 1940–45*. London: Cassell, 1966.

Townsend, Peter. *Time and Chance*. London: Collins, 1978. Author was with 43 Squadron at Tangmere; with 85 Squadron at Debden in the Battle of Britain. After the war he was the royal equerry with whom Princess Margaret, the Queen's sister, renounced marriage. See also his *Duel of Eagles* and *Duel in the Dark*.

Turner, J. F. *VCs of the Air*. London: Harrap, 1960.

Walker, O. *Sailor Malan*. London: Cassell, 1953.

Ward-Thomas, Pat. *Not only Golf*. London: Hodder and Stoughton, 1981. Autobiography.

Wright, Esther Terry. *Pilot's Wife's Tale*. London: Bodley Head, 1942.

BLITZ: THE GERMAN FOLLOW-UP TO THE BATTLE OF BRITAIN

Fraser, David. *Blitz*. London: Macmillan, 1979. See FICTION.

Lee, Asher. *Blitz on Britain*. London: Four Square.

Macmillan, Harold. *The Blast of War, 1939–45*. London: Harper and Row, 1967.

Price, Alfred. *Blitz on Britain*. London: Ian Allan, 1977.

BOMBERS

Although it is primarily fighter aircraft which were involved in the Battle, some consideration should be given by the researcher to Bomber Command, if only because it had been thought they were the first essential. "The bomber will always get through" was a famous statement, made without thought that bombers needed fighter escort for protection and that the first line of a modern country's defence is its fighter strength. Bombers, in the early stages of the war, dropped a considerable amount of leaflets on Germany, warning its people of what they were up against and into what they were being led. Doubtless such leaflets were all written off as propaganda similar to their own, against which they were helpless. That fighter aircraft could also be bombers was still in the future. Bomber crews flew many daily/nightly operational raids into Germany during the fraught months of the Battle.

Cheshire, Gp Capt Leonard. *Bomber Pilot*. London: Hutchinson, 1943.

Gee, J. W. *Wingspan.* Reminiscences of a bomber pilot, 99 and 153 Sqns.
Hodgson, J. R. A. *Letters from a Bomber Pilot.* London: Methuen, 1985.

BOOKSHOPS

Air Collect, 184 Wellington Hill West, Henleaze, Bristol BS9 4QP.

Anglo-German Book Service, 44 Cornfield Terrace, St. Leonards on Sea, Essex.

Aviation and Maritime Bookroom, Robert Humm and Co., Station House, Stamford, Lincolnshire PE9 2JN.

Aviation and Military Books, Midland Counties Publications, 24 The Hollow, Earl Shilton, Leicester LE9 7NA. Has good catalogue with publishers' listings, videos, badges, medals, calendars, etc., books on military history. Warehouse is at 3 Land Society Lane. Browsing invited.

Aviation Antiques, 369 Croydon Rd., Caterham, Surrey.

Aviation Bookshop, 656 Holloway Road, London N19 3PD. Has an excellent collection of books, magasines and memorabilia. Contact Dave Hatherell.

Brian Cocks, 18 Woodgate, Helpston, Peterborough PE6 7ED. Visitors by appointment.

Crawford-Peters Aeronautics, 37127 Nassau Drive, San Diego, Calif. 92115.

Falconwood Transport and Military Bookshop, 5 Falconwood Parade, The Green, Wallington, Kent DA16 2PL.

Hearts of Oak Bookshop, 63 High Street, Rochester, Kent.

Motor Books 33 (FP), St Martins Court, London WC2N 4AL.

Phillimore and Co. Ltd., Shopwyke Hall, Oving, Nr Chichester, W Sussex PO20 6BQ. Books on local history, particularly of the area. What was RAF Tangmere is just down the road. In this house and at Shopwyke House, now a school, officers from Tangmere were billeted when bombed out in August 1940.

Pickering and Co., 42 The Shambles, York, Yorkshire YO1 2LR. At the top of the shop is a collection of secondhand flying books in a room called The Cockpit. Shop has connections with Yorkshire Air Museum at nearby Elvington.

Hay on Wye is a village in Herefordshire, totally dedicated to books. Among its many bookshops there are two good ones for militaria, including a wide selection of aviation titles. Stock varies weekly. As in the case of art galleries, many more bookshops can be located by consulting the back pages of most flying magasines, but care should be taken to verify that the addresses are still correct.

Mail order is another way in which books of this nature will probably be found. Many must now be sought secondhand, since most are long out of print. An example of such a service is Terry Smith, Balwyn House, The Common, Freethorpe, Norwich, NR13 3LX. Similar lists are available from other mail order services. Publishers are not always given, but condition and price are stated and reasonable.

CANADA

Drew, G. A. *Canada's Fighting Airmen.* Maclean, 1931. Personal detail.
Field, Peter J. Canada's Wings. London: John Lane, Bodley Head, 1942.
Halliday, Hugh. *The Canadian Years.* Ottawa: Canadian War Museum.
Kostenuk/Griffin. *RCAF Squadrons.* Ottawa: S. Stevens, 1977.
Lowe, Frank. *Among the Few: Canada's Airmen in the Battle of Britain.* Ottawa: RCAF Historical Section, 1948. *Among the Few* also at PRO in AIR 20/7346.
———. "Twenty Years Ago They Broke the Luftwaffe." *Montreal Star Weekend Magasine,* 10 September 1960.
Milberry, Larry. *The Canadian Air Force.*
———. *Sixty Years.* The RCAF and CF Air Command, 1924–84.
Peden, Murray. *A Thousand Shall Fall.* London: Imperial War Museum, 1981; Ontario: Canada's Wings Inc., 1982.
Shores, Christopher. *History of the Royal Canadian Air Force.* London: Bison Books, 1984. Good pictures, index and squadron listings.
See also John Terraine, *The Right of the Line.*

CHILDREN'S BOOKS

Beal, George, ed. *Flight: The Quizzer Book.* Martin C. Sharp, consultant. London: Owlet Books, 1975.
Callaway, Tim. *A Battle of Britain Project Book.* London: Headway, Hodder and Stoughton, 1989.
Collier, Basil. *The Battle of Britain.* London: Jackdaw Publications, Jonathan Cape, 1969.
How it Works: The Aeroplane. Loughborough: Ladybird.
The Ladybird Book of Aircraft. Loughborough: Ladybird, Wills and Hepworth.
Our Wonderful Air Force. Elementary encyclopedia.
The Story of Flight. Loughborough: Ladybird, Wills and Hepworth,.
Taylor, John W. R. *The Airman in the Royal Air Force.* Loughborough: Wills and Hepworth, 1967. Illustrated by John Berry. Ladybird Easy Reading Book. People at Work series.
———. *The Royal Air Force.* Oxford: Oxford University Press, 1965. Illustrations by Victor Ambrus. Historical account for children.
Tilbury, Ann. *The Battle of Britain.* London: Simon and Schuster, 1990. Reprint of the 1981 edition with illustrations by Michael Turner, President, Guild of Aviation Artists.

COLLECTIONS

The Aeroplane Collection, Warmington Craft Workshops, 4 miles north of Crewe. Address correspondence regarding visits to 54 Lee Avenue, Altrincham, Cheshire WA14 5HR.

Douglas Arnold's Warbirds of Great Britain, Bitteswell Airfield, Lutterworth, Leices. Admission by prior permission. Originally at Blackbushe; may be moved again. Spits, Hurricanes and Messerschmitt.

Battle of Britain Memorial Flight, RAF Coningsby, to where application to visit should be made. This is a demonstration flight of well maintained but veteran aircraft which actually took part. It has its own crew and archive, and takes part as a whole or in sections in memorials and anniversaries.

Brencham Historic Aircraft Collection, Hurn Airport Bournemouth, Christchurch, Dorset. Prior permission only, telephone 0202 580909.

Cherwell Collection at Nuffield College, Oxford. Lord Cherwell was Professor Frederick Lindermann, scientific adviser to Sir Winston Churchill.

Holloway Collection. See section below.

Imperial War Museum, Lambeth, London SE 1, and Duxford Airfield, Cambridgeshire, CB2 4QR. Open daily March to October, 10:30 A.M. to 5:30 P.M. Includes the Lindsey Walton Collection and new Battle of Britain videos with related aircraft, one of which is Noel Agazarian's Spitfire.

Old Flying Machine Company, Duxford Airfield, Cambridgeshire. [Ex-Red Arrow leader Ray Hanna bought a Spitfire IX, one of the few still flying, which flew in WW2, shot down an FW190 and a Bf 109, whilst with 222 Sqn from Hornchurch. Thus was the collection formed in 1983. Aircraft used in the TV film *Piece of Cake.*

Old Warden Aerodrome. See Shuttleworth Collection, below.

Nigel Ponsford Collection, 94 Park Land Drive, Leeds LS6 4 P2. Prior permission, 0532 691564.

RAF Museum, Hendon, north London

Science Museum, Kensington, London.

Shuttleworth Collection, Old Warden Aerodrome, Biggleswade, Bedfordshire, SG 18 9EP. Closed one week at Christmas, otherwise 10:30 to 17:30. Dates from 1920 when Richard Shuttleworth built his workshops on family estate. Includes a Gloster Gladiator which was used by only one squadron—247—in the Battle of Britain.

Strathallan Aircraft Collection, Strathallan Airfield, Auchterarder, Perthshire, Scotland. April to October daily 10:00-17:00; off the B8062, west of Kinkell Bridge.

Ken Woolley Collection, Berkswell Forge, Berkswell, Coventry, CV7 7BB. Prior permission only. 5 miles west of Coventry. Miscellaneous, memorabilia, photographs, components.

It is advisable to check with each before visiting, as there have been many amalgamations and changes. For full details of these and more, see Gordon Riley, *Vintage Aircraft Directory* (Bourne End: Aston Publications, 1985) and Bob Ogden, *British Aviation Museums and Collections* (Stamford, Lincolnshire: Key Publishing, 1986).

Collection of Flight Lieutenant John Holloway

Soon after the war was over *Flight Lieutenant John Holloway* started to collect the signatures of all the aircrew of Fighter Command who had fought in the Battle. It was a labour of love that took many years to assemble, right up to his death. From them he made a series of presentation volumes from signatures collected not only from the survivors themselves, but from the passports, log books, identity cards, letters and the like of those who did not come back. It makes a unique memorial which may be seen at the Imperial War Museum.

Flt Lt Holloway was stationed at Kenley in 1955 in 615 Squadron when the film *Reach for the Sky* was being made, and the completed list was presented to the Museum in October 1969. A similar list with amendations and additions was compiled by Sqn Ldr F. E. Dymond and called *They Fell in the Battle.* This can be seen at the RAF Museum at Hendon. A tableau based on these memorials was presented to the Smithsonian Institute on 15 September 1976.

The complete Roll of Honour of the Battle is in the RAF Memorial Chapel in Westminster Abbey, near to the Memorial Window. For details see *Flight* magasine for 1947 and the book by Winston G. Ramsey, ed., *The Battle of Britain, Then and Now.*

When Flt Lt Holloway died, Mr. and Mrs. E. Murray of 1 Carew Close, Old Couldson, Surrey, undertook to answer any questions and add further research. Enquiries should be made to them direct.

COLLECTIONS ON BATTLE OF BRITAIN AIRFIELDS

Aces High Flying Museum, at North Weald. Correspondence to Fairoaks Airport, Chobham, Surrey, GU24 8HX. Open at selected times in the summer. North Weald is 2 miles northeast of Epping on B181. Formed by Mike Woodley in 1979 to specialise in aircraft for films and TV.

Military Aviation Museum, Tangmere, Chichester, West Sussex P020 6ER. Admission 11:00–17:30 daily, March through November. Signposted off the A27, 3 miles east of Chichester. Closed as an RAF station in 1972, this was one of the most famous fighter bases—the modern Agincourt. Opened 1982; half the museum is devoted to the Battle of Britain.

RAF Battle of Britain Memorial Flight at RAF Marham, Lincolnshire LN4 1AA. Prior application for guided tours, 0526 42581. 13 miles northeast of Sleaford on A153. Hurricanes, Spitfires, Lancasters, etc. The Flight had been at Martlesham Heath and North Weald after originally at Biggin Hill. All Battle of Britain stations. The aircraft are painted in the colours which honour the squadrons serving in the Battle.

RAF Exhibition Flight, RAF Abingdon, Oxfordshire, tel. 0235 21288. Prior arrangement necessary. 2 miles northwest of Abingdon off the B4017. 71 Maintenance Unit was originally responsible for these aircraft. Spitfires and others.

See also the two museum guides listed in the COLLECTIONS section by Gordon Riley and Bob Ogden.

CZECHOSLOVAKIA

There are numerous books written in the Czech language about Czechs in the RAF. For information about this it would be best to contact Sqn Ldr Marcel

Ludikar of Northwood, West London, or via the Czechoslovak Club, 74 West End Lane, London NW6 1SX. He is the keeper of the archives of the Aviators' Association.

Benes, Bohus. *Wings in Exile.* Czechoslovak Independent Weekly, 1942. English/Czech text.

Capka, Joe. *Red Sky at Night.* London: Antony Blond, 1958. Czech pilot in 68 night fighter squadron.

Darlington, Roger. *Night Hawk.* London: William Kimber, 1985. English text. About Karel Kuttelwascher, DFC, night intruder ace, by his son-in-law. This book has a full bibliography of books that mention the subject's name, as well as a general bibliography in English and Czech, and an overview of the situation in Czechoslovakia. The pilot was in No. 1 Squadron. See also Czechoslovak Club above.

Kanadske Listy. Czech-language newspaper which specialises in keeping in touch with former aviators. Published in Canada.

Loucky, F. *Mnozi Nedoleteli* (Did Not Make It). Prague, 1989. About 511 Squadron.

DATABASES

BLAISE Line, Marketing Office, The British Library, Bibliographic Services Division, 2 Sheraton Street, London W1V 4BH.

DIALOG Information Retrieval Service, P.O. Box 8, Abingdon, Oxford OX13 6EG. Has Book Review Index; Biography Master Index.

LC Marc. Books published since 1968.

LC Marc. American Library of Congress, also included in BLAISE Line.

Remarc. Books before 1968. From the American Library of Congress.

UK Marc. Main catalogue of the British Library.

For registered British Library users it is possible to order LOAN copies while on line to BLAISE. For more information on these data bases—though not related to the Battle of Britain—see Ray Hammond, *The Writer and the Word Processor* (London and New York: Coronet, 1984). For other data bases to be used with different computer makes, refer to back pages and classified ads of computer and flying magasines.

DATES

The Annual Register. On the open shelves at the PRO.

Collier, Richard. *1940: The World in Flames.* London: Hamish Hamilton, 1979; Penguin, 1980.

Fyson, Nance Lui. *The 1940s: Portrait of a Decade.* London: Batsford, 1988. Mostly about the United States, but has good pictures of London during the Battle of Britain.

The Royal Institute of International Affairs. *Chronology of the Second World War.* Lon-

don: The Institute, annual. A day-by-day account of the Second World War, with 1940 in close detail.
Stevenson, William. *A Man Called Intrepid.* London: Macmillan, 1976. Has good chronological date pages.
The Times Index. Available in most larger libraries, or the British Library, or the PRO's Library.
Waugh, Evelyn. *Put Out More Flags.* London: Hutchinson, 1968. A novel of the 1940s.

Newspapers of the period are housed at the Newspaper Library, Colindale, N. London, where there are long runs of the local, county, and world presses from their first printing. Local newspapers may also be located in central reference libraries of the town concerned. See also EVENTS section.

DEFENCE

The Air Defence of Great Britain. 6 vols. Available at PRO/Kew. Vol. 1, AIR 41/14, 1936–40; Vol. 2, AIR 41/15, Battle of Britain; Vol. 3, AIR 41/17, June 1940–41; Vol. 4, AIR 41/18, 1940–41; Vol. 5, AIR 41/19; Vol. 6, AIR 41/55.
Collier, Basil. *Defence of the United Kingdom.* London: HMSO, 1957.
Ellis, John. *Social History of the Machine Gun.* London: Croom Helm.

See also AIR DEFENCE OF GREAT BRITAIN section.

EAGLE SQUADRONS

These were RAF squadrons staffed by volunteer American pilots, though the composition of their ground crews was not necessarily American. Initially, until sufficient personnel were trained, the commanding officer, at least, of the first Eagle Squadron, 71, was British.

Gradually two other squadrons were formed whose aircrew was entirely American. Though these were not in existence until the Battle of Britain was over, some did come into being in time for the Blitz toward the end of 1940. Many Americans were already in the RAF, as can be seen from a study of the fighter OTUs. A great many stayed in the RAF, though at considerably lower pay, when in December 1941 the United States came into the war. In the main those in the Eagle Squadrons had joined before 1942 and on that date were transferred to the USAAF as soon as its units were on British soil.

The PRO references are 71 Squadron, AIR 27/623, formed September 1940; 121 Squadron, AIR 27/914, formed May 1941; 133 Squadron, AIR 27/945, formed August 1941.

The bases on which they were stationed should also be searched, by name, in AIR 28. They were disbanded in 1942 and most of their personnel absorbed into the USAAF.

71 was an old RAF number reissued, originally an RFC Squadron formed in 1917 with Australians. It was reformed at Church Fenton as the first Eagle Squadron and the only one to fight in the Battle of Britain. No Spitfires were

produced by the United States, but about 600 were supplied and operating in U.S. service as part of the reverse Lease-Lend Plan. They wore American insignia. Many British future RAF pilots were also trained in America before 1942 as part of the same scheme.

71 Squadron flew Hurricanes until 20 August 1941, when they were converted to Spitfires. The other two Squadrons flew Spitfires exclusively. When the 31st and 52nd Fighter Groups USAAF arrived in Britain, they too flew Spitfires. When the Eagle Squadrons left the RAF and joined the 8th Air Force, they became the 4th Fighter Group's 334, 335 and 336 Squadrons, based variously in the south of England, then in Europe.

Technical information for these aircraft and squadrons can be found in Gordon Swanborough and Peter A. Bowers, *United States Military Aircraft since 1909* (London: Putnam, 1963; new ed. 1989.)

For other Americans in the RAF, for example, see CFS Upavon, AIR 29/604, at PRO, for September 1940. CFS was Central Flying School, but there may have been other Americans in Operational Training Units, AIR 29. Certainly there were some at Annan, in AIR 29/682, and at 23 OTU Pershore, AIR 29/667. See also AMERICANS section and ATA.

Haughland, Vern. *The Eagle Squadrons: Yanks in the RAF 1940–42*. Newton Abbot, Devon: David and Charles, 1960; New York: Ziff Flying Books, 1978. A journalist's useful account, with good documentation, but watch for errors about Billy Fiske, first American to be killed in the Battle.

Kelly, Terence. *Hurricane and Spitfire Pilots at War*. London: William Kimber, 1986.

Kennerley, Byron. *The Eagles Roar*. Washington, D.C.: Zenger Publishing, 1941, 1980. A first-hand personal experience of the end of the Battle of Britain period and of Americans in the RAF. Although American names are mentioned, place names are not, and there are few RAF names which might lead to identification. This can be clarified by checking the 71 Squadron records in the AIR 27 class at the PRO.

Wilson, Eunice. "An American in the RAF." *Nostalgia, no. 6* (October 1989). Corrects the error about Billy Fiske.

ESCAPES AND EVASIONS

Brickill, Paul. *Escape or Die*. London: Evans Brothers, 1952. Authentic stories of the Escaping Society.

———. *Escape to Danger*. With Conrad Norton. London: Faber and Faber, 1946.

———. *The Great Escape*. London: Faber, 1963.

Burt, Kendal, and James Leasor. *The One That Got Away*. London: Collins with Michael Joseph, 1956. German Air Ace Franz von Werra, shot down 5 December 1940 by Flt Lt John Webster, 41 Squadron, over Kent. PoW, made amazing escape to Canada and back to Germany.

Cooper, Alan W. *Free to Fight Again, 1940–45*. London: William Kimber, 1988. RAF escapes and evasions. Several well-known names, members of the RAF Escaping

Society, interviewed. Link this book with *Turncoat* by Brendan Murphy. Good index, brief bibliography, PRO references.
Crawley, Aiden. *Escapes from Germany*. London: Collins, 1956.
Emms, G. "Investigation No. 1." *After the Battle Magasine*, No. 35.
Evans, A. J. *Escape and Liberation 1940–45*. London: Hodder and Stoughton, 1945.
Furniss-Roe, Bill. *Believed Safe*. London: William Kimber, 1987.
Jackson, R. *A Taste of Freedom*. London: A. Barker, 1964.
McLaughlin, I. "The Nearly Great Escape." *Fly Past* (August 1987).
Murphy, Brendan. *Turncoat*. London: Macdonald, 1987. Story of the traitor Harold Cole. Excellent bibliography and notes on Battle of Britain and 1940 in general. Unfortunately gives few RAF names, but does mention George Barclay, author of *Fighter Pilot*. Cross reference with *Saturday at MI9* by Airey Neave.
Neave, Airey. *Saturday at MI9*. London: Hodder and Stoughton, 1969. History of the underground escape lines in Europe 1940–45, by one of the organisers, who was himself later shot in London.
Nesbitt, Roy Conyers. *Failed to Return*. London: William Kimber, 1988.
RAF Escaping Society. 206 Brompton Road, London SW.
Reid, P. R. *My Favourite Escape Stories*. London: Lutterworth Press, 1975. Contains the story of Wg Cdr Basil Embry, RAF, and of Oberleutnant Franz von Werra, Luftwaffe. For the latter, see also Wentzel, *Single or Return?*
Richardson, Anthony. *Wingless Victory*. London: Odhams, 1950. As told to Richardson by Sir Basil Embry about the summer of 1940.
Spiller, Herbert J. *Ticket to Freedom*. Survivor of a Halifax crash in France, and escaped.
Vanderstock, Bob. *War Pilot of Orange*. Holland. Fighter pilot in Stalag Luft 111, one of those who escaped when 50 prisoners were shot. 322 Sq, CO at war's end.
Wentzel, Fritz. *Single or Return?* London: William Kimber.

PRO references: AIR 20, AIR 8, AIR 40/268 and WO/208, and the RAF Escaping Society in AIR 8/1423. Escapers and Evaders, on their return to the UK, were interrogated by MI9 at Rooms 303 and 386 in the Grand Central Hotel, Marylebone, London, which is still there. Originally it belonged to the Great Western Railway. It is no longer a hotel.

ESPIONAGE

Brown, Anthony Cave. *Bodyguard of Lies*. London: Comet, 1986.
Collier, Basil. *Hidden Weapons*. London: Hamish Hamilton, 1982. Allied secret and undercover services in WW2. Useful chapter on 1940. (Basil Collier worked during the Battle of Britain and the Blitz in the ops room of Fighter Command HQ at Bentley Priory. He used Ultra material from Bletchley and later returned to Fighter Command as Air Historical Officer.)
Foot, M.R.D. *SOE: The Special Operations Executive, 1940–45*. London: BBC, 1984.
HMSO. *British Intelligence in the Second World War*. London: HMSO, 1979. Excellent chapter on the Battle of Britain.
Jones, R.V. *Most Secret War*. London: Hamish Hamilton, 1978.
Lewin, Ronald. *Ultra Goes to War: The Secret Story*. London: Hutchinson, 1978. Good bibliography and chapter notes. See also INTELLIGENCE, EVIDENCE AND OBSERVATION section.

West, Nigel. *MI6: British Secret Intelligence Service Operations, 1909–45*. London: Weidenfeld and Nicolson, 1983.

———. *A Matter of Trust*: MI5, 1945–72. London.

West, Nigel, and Richard Deacon. *Spy*. London: BBC, 1980.

EVENTS

In addition to those already listed and the aids mentioned, there are many chronological lists of events in which WW2 and the Battle of Britain are detailed day by day. They include *The Annual Register; Chronology of the Second World War; Keatings Contemporary Archives; London Gazette;* and *The Times Index*. Reference libraries will have other similar sources.

FAMILY HISTORY AND RAF GENEALOGY

Researching these subjects is not easy, though in the *Battle of Britain, Then and Now* will be found many kinships and family connections among those who died as well as those who survived. Many RAF families are dynastic, and present RAF pilots are often the grandsons of WW1 RFC pilots, and sons of the RAF themselves, so that the same names occur in several generations. For example, Flt Lt William Rhodes-Moorhouse, DFC, b. 1914, was the only son of 2nd Lt William Barnard Rhodes-Moorhouse, the first VC of the air, who died in hospital in 1915, one year after his son was born. William Jr., 601 Squadron, was lost in 1940 in September at Tangmere.

His brother-in-law, Flt Lt Richard Demetriadi, was missing the month before from the same squadron led by Rhodes-Moorhouse. He is buried in France.

The 16th Baronet Sir John Augustus Hope died in 1924 when his son Philip was aged twelve. Flt Lt Sir Philip Archibald Hope, DFC, as he was to become, died in July 1987; he had also commanded this famous 601 Squadron. He was married in 1938 to Ruth Davis, whose brother Carl was born of American parents in South Africa and was killed in 1940. Mementoes of both are to be found in Tangmere's Aviation Museum.

Another 601 Squadron pilot was Loel Guinness, who died in January 1989, aged 82, as a Group Captain ret'd. He was the son of a banker, of the well known Guinness family, and served in the Battle of Britain at Tangmere.

Most of these names can be checked through *Debrett, Burke's Peerage,* and *The Complete Peerage,* but do not neglect the obituaries in the *Daily Telegraph* and *The Times*, as well as cross referencing with many of the squadron histories available, and the squadron operational record in AIR 27 at the PRO.

Ordinary birth certificates may be obtained for those born in England and Wales from St Catherine's House, Aldwych, London; present cost, £6.00 each; no search fee if done in person. For those born in Scotland or Ireland searches must be made in the corresponding registrar's office of each country. These will give the name of the father, mother, address where born and the registration district.

Death certificates are also available for those who died in or over the UK, but not if beyond British territorial waters. There is an Index of War Deaths at St. Catherine's which gives service number and squadron or unit. Those of unknown graves will be found on the Runnymede Memorial, Staines; these and those with accessible graves can be found through the Commonwealth and Allied War Graves Commission. For the Runnymede names there are no death certificates, though parents' names and home address are often listed. Occasionally others may be found in consular records at St Catherine's House. Church burial registers may yield some information.

For genealogical information, go to the Society of Genealogists, 14 Charterhouse Buildings, London, for further advice, or to the County Record office in the relevant county. The reference section of public libraries will be able to help with local cemeteries and churchyards.

Family History in the RAF

If you doubt that two main interests can be joined, read the book *Fighter Pilot*, a self-portrait by George Barclay, DFC, who learned to fly with the Cambridge University Air Squadron at Duxford in 1939. In September of that year he was living at 67 Jesus Lane, Cambridge, and his family at Cromer Vicarage in Norfolk. That family consisted of his two brothers, two sisters, and his parents, Rev. G. A. Barclay and his wife Dorothy. George was at Trinity, unsure of what he wanted to be, but with a desire to be a mercenary like his ancestors Col. David Barclay, who served the seventeenth-century King Gustav of Sweden in the Thirty Years War, and General Barclay de Tolly, who commanded the Russian army in its retreat before Napoleon at Moscow. But there was another pull, toward being a missionary like his grandfather, who had been converted by the Americans Moody and Sankey as a result of serving in China, India and the Belgian Congo. Col. David became a Quaker, and all the Barclays come from a long linking connection with the bankers and statesmen of the Gurney, Wedgwood, Hanbury and other interrelated families. (See *Friends and Relations* by Verily Anderson, and *The Wedgwood Circle* by Barbara and Hensleigh Wedgwood.) George, the RAF pilot, had obviously done his family history. Called up as were all the RAFVR on 1 September 1939, Sgt 754320 became Pilot Officer George Barclay 74661 on 1 October and was posted to No. 3 Initial Training Wing, Marine Court, Hastings, along with so many other young men destined to become aircrew. The book, based on his diaries, tells of his posting to 249 Squadron at Leconfield, later to North Weald and the Battle of Britain, and finally, past two shootings down, the DFC and his last battle over El Alamein in July 1942, where, as a Squadron Leader, he was killed.

Barclay, R. A. George, DFC. *Fighter Pilot*. London: William Kimber, 1976. A self-portrait edited by Dr Humphrey Wynn. Foreword by Sir John Grandy, GCB KBE DSO, then CO of 249 Squadron, in which Barclay served during the Battle of

Britain at Leconfield and North Weald. Good map, index, bibliography and abbreviations list. See also Wynn, below.

Wynn, Dr. Humphrey. *Royal Air Force Quarterly* (September 1974). Article commemorates the Battle. Author was an Air Historical Branch of MoD historian.

FICTION

Bates, H. E. *The Greatest People in the World*. London: Transworld Publishers, 1952. Short stories written by Flying Officer X.

———. *How Sleep the Brave*. London: Transworld Publishers, 1952. Short stories written as Flying Officer X.

Beaty, David, and Betty Beaty. *Wings of the Morning*. London: Macmillan, 1982. A novel about flying from 1903 to 1981; good section on 1939 to 1945.

Blake, (pseud.). *Readiness at Dawn*. London: Digit Books, Brown Watson. Author was a Controller in the Ops Room at Hornchurch. Fictionalised account of the Battle from first-hand personal experience. Pseudonym of Sqn Ldr Ronald Adams.

Eagle, Robert, and Herbie Knott. *How They Made the Film "Piece of Cake."* Boxtree, 1988.

Fraser, David. *Blitz*. London: Macmillan, 1979. Although primarily about a later period, it has good opening details about the Battle of Britain and the construction of Churchill's wartime HQ in Pall Mall, called The Annexe.

Henrey, Madeleine. *London under Fire (1940–45)*. London: J. M. Dent, 1969. A French girl living in London during the Battle of Britain.

———. *Madeleine, Young Wife*. London: J. M. Dent, 1969. War and peace on a farm in Normandy, before and after the war.

Kuniczak, W. S. *Valedictory*. London: Michael Joseph, 1984. Fictionalised semi-documentary about a Polish squadron in the Battle of Britain. Useful facts about Poland.

Moyes, Patricia. *Johnny Underground*. London: Collins, 1965. A Crime Club novel about a Battle of Britain pilot. Quotes John Pudney's poem "Johnny Head in Air."

Robinson, Derek. *Piece of Cake*. London: Hamish Hamilton, 1983; Pan, 1984. This was made into the 1988 TV film which caused great controversy about its accuracy. It *is* fiction, but was being judged as a documentary, which it was not intended to be. Max Hastings praised it.

Slee, Daphne. *The Poor Wise Man*. London: Peter Davies, 1952. Love story of a test pilot on an AMES unit (Air Ministry Experimental Station).

Trevor, Elleston. *Squadron Airborne*. London: Heinemann, 1955; Pan Battle of Britain series, 1957. A fast moving story of The Few, there is a good glossary included.

Waugh, Evelyn. *Put Out More Flags*. London: Methuen, 1982. A novel of the 1940s.

Many factual accounts, such as Paul Brickhill's *Reach for the Sky*, about Douglas Bader, were fictionalised into film and later into TV film. These are worth looking at, but as fiction, since they are only substantially accurate. They are often repeated on TV around Battle of Britain Day, 15 September.

FIGHTERS (MISCELLANEOUS EXPERIENCES)

Austin, A. B. *Fighter Command.* London, 1941.

Baker, E.C.R. *Fighter Aces of the RAF.* London: William Kimber, 1962.

Batchelor, Jack, and Chris Chant. *Fighter.* Devon: David and Charles, 1988.

Beamont, Roland. *My Part of the Sky.* Wellingborough: Patrick Stephens, 1989. The much decorated pilot who became a Wing Cdr at the age of 23, later to be chief test pilot for English Electric and the first to fly fighter jets. No index, no bibliography, but good pictures. See also his *Fighter Test Pilot, Testing Years,* and *Phoenix into Ashes.*

Brickhill, Paul. *Reach for the Sky.* London: Collins, 1954. Life story of Douglas Bader.

Bowyer, Chaz. *The Beaufighter at War.* London: William Kimber, 1987.

———. *Fighter Command 1936–68.* London: J. M. Dent, 1980. Has good list of squadron disposition.

———. *Fighter Pilots of the RAF 1939–45.* London: William Kimber, 1980.

Braham, J.R.D. *Scramble.* London: William Kimber, 1961, 1987.

Brookes, Andrew J. *Fighter Squadron at War.* London: Ian Allan.

Burn, Michael. *Spitfire! Spitfire!* Dorset: Blandford Press.

Cooper, Bryan, and John Batchelor. *Fighter.* London: Macdonald, 1974.

Darlington, Roger. *Night Hawk.* London: William Kimber, 1985. About Karel Kuttelwascher, DFC, Czech Battle of Britain fighter pilot, by his son-in-law.

Dundas, Sir Hugh. *Flying Start: A Fighter Pilot's War Years.* London: Stanley Paul, 1988.

Franks, Norman L. *Hurricane at War 2.* London: Ian Allan, 1986.

———. *Scramble to Victory: Five Fighter Pilots.* London: William Kimber, 1987. 1939–45.

———. *Sky Tiger.* London: William Kimber, 1980. About Sailor Malan.

———. *Valiant Wings.* London: William Kimber, 1988. Battle and Blenheim Squadrons over France, 1940. The following are also by this author but not necessarily all about the Battle of Britain: *The Air Battle of Dunkirk*; *The Air Battle of Imphal*; *Conflict over the Bay*; *Double Mission*; *Fighter Leader*; *The Greatest Air Battle*; *Spitfires over the Arakan*; *Typhoon Attack*; and *Wings of Freedom.*

Furniss-Roe, Bill. *Believed Safe.* London: William Kimber, 1987. Of 66 Squadron, an evader.

Green, William, and Gordon Swanborough. *Fighters, an Illustrated Anatomy of the World's Aircraft.* London: Salamander, 1981.

Gunston, Bill. *British Fighters of World War II.* Airbooks Warehouse.

———. *Fighter Pilots of the RAF, 1939–1945.* London: William Kimber, 1980. Updated and reprinted, 1984.

———. *Fighters in Classic Aircraft Series.* Feltham: Hamlyn, 1978.

Johnstone, Sandy. *Adventures in the Sky.* London: William Kimber, 1978.

———. *Enemy in the Sky: My 1940 Diary.* London: William Kimber, 1976.

———. *Spitfire into Battle.* London: William Kimber.

———. *Where No Angels Dwell.* London: Jarrolds, 1969.

Kelly, Terence. *Hurricane and Spitfire Pilots at War.* London: William Kimber, 1986.

Lucas, Laddie. *Flying Colours.* London: Hutchinson, 1981.

Mackenzie, Wing Cdn K. W. *Hurricane Combat.* London: William Kimber, 1988. About 501 and 247 Squadrons.

MacKersey, Ian. "Tally Ho! Cried John Peel." *RAF Flying Review* 5, No. 2.

Offenberg, Jean. *Lonely Warrior.* First Eng. ed., London: Souvenir Press, 1956; Granada Mayflower, 1969. A Belgian pilot in the Battle of Britain.

Oxspring, Gp Capt Bobby. *Spitfire Command.* London: William Kimber, 1984.

Price, Alfred. *Spitfire at War.* London: Ian Allan.

———. *Spitfire at War 2.* London: Ian Allan.

———. *The Spitfire Story.* London: William Kimber.

Rawlings, J. J. D. *Fighter Squadrons of the RAF.* London: Macdonald, 1969.

Rawnsley, C. F., and Robert Wright. *Night Fighter.* London: Collins, 1957.

Robertson, Bruce. *Spitfire: The story of the Famous Fighter.* London: Arms and Armour Press, 1962.

Skinner, Michael. *Red Flag.* London: William Kimber. Training for fighter pilots.

Stewart, Adrian. *Hurricane.* London: William Kimber, 1982.

Stokes, Douglas. *Fighting in the Air.* London: William Kimber. Official combat techniques for British fighter pilots.

———. *Biography. Paddy Finucane: Fighter Ace.* London: William Kimber, 1983.

———. *Wings Aflame.* London: William Kimber, 1984. Biography of Gp Capt Victor Beamish DSO DFC AFC.

Townsend, Peter. *Duel in the Dark.* London: Harrap, 1986.

———. *Duel of Angels.* London: Harrap, 1986.

Wykeham, Peter, AVM. *Fighter Command.* London: Putnam, 1960.

Wynn, H., ed. *Fighter Pilot.* London: William Kimber, 1976.

FILMS

Angels One Five. Associated British Pathé film made in 1952; set in Kent during the Battle of Britain. Semi-documentary. Good shots, but the affected speech film makers mistakenly thought everyone used spoils it now. Revived 1989. Angels sometimes referred to the enemy, but mostly it was the code name for the height at which the enemy was seen or the RAF fighters were to fly. It was a code related to the height of the day and instructions were altered daily. Calculated in feet by 1,000. Thus Angels 10 equal 10,000 feet.

Battle of Britain. LWT in series Theatre of War, 1969. Repeated 3 September 1989 for 50th anniversary. Directed by Guy Hamilton. Ron Goodwin's music.

Dangerous Moonlight. Film about a Polish pilot, starring Anton Walbrook. The music for this film was *The Warsaw Concerto* by Richard Addinsell.

Missing. BBC TV film. Story of Hugh Beresford, killed 7 September 1940. His aircraft's recovery and his reburial at Brookwood Cemetery in Surrey was undertaken by Wealden Aviation Archaelogical Group. See *The Battle of Britain, Then and Now*, by Winston G. Ramsey, ed.

Piece of Cake. A film for television made from the book of the same title by Derek Robinson. The controversial story of a British fighter squadron in the Battle of Britain. This was not a documentary, though adverse reviewers described it as such.

Reach for the Sky. A film made from the book of the same title by Paul Brickhill. Describes the life of Douglas Bader.

There are many more. For best guidance look in the contemporary film magasines of the period at the Newspaper Library at Colindale, north London. A branch of the British Library, it is in the same road as the RAF Museum.

There are also films available at the British Film Institute and the National Film Archive, 21 Stephen Street, London W1.

See also the National Sound Archive, 29 Exhibition Road, Kensington, London.

GENERAL

Articles of War. *In Spectator Book of World War II.* London: Grafton, 1989.

Baldwin, Hanson W. *The Crucial Years, 1939–41.* London: Weidenfeld and Nicolson, 1976. Parts of this book appeared first in the *New York Times.* Good chapter and source notes. Good Battle of Britain chapter.

Holmes, Richard. *World Atlas of Warfare.* London: Michael Beazley, 1988. 1940 origins of the word *Blitzkreig,* as compared with names for other and previous battles (Chapter 12). Military innovations that changed the course of history. Good index and bibliography.

Terraine, John. *The Right of the Line.* London: Hodder and Stoughton, 1985; Sceptre, 1988. The RAF in the European War, 1939–45. Part 3 has 50 pages on the Battle. Very good appendices, abbreviations, General and RAF Index and Aircraft Index; extensive bibliography and chapter notes. Invaluable work of reference.

GERMANS—THE OTHER SIDE

Ansel, Walter. *Hitler Confronts England.* Durham, N.C.: Duke University Press, 1960.

Barbas, Bernd. *Planes of the Luftwaffe Fighter Aces.* Germany.

Baumbach, Werner. "Why We Lost." *RAF News* 7, no. 12 (1952–53).

———. *Broken Swastika.* London: Robert Hale.

Baur, Lt Gen Hans. *Hitler's Pilot.* London: Frederick Muller, 1950, 1958. See also the controversial report in PRO AIR/619 and Germany in AIR 55. See also details of German Deserters at the PRO in AIR 16. Enemy aircraft crashes in UK are included.

Bekker, Cajus. The Luftwaffe War Diaries. London: Macdonald, 1967.

Bloemertz, G. *Heaven Next Stop.* 1953. A German fighter pilot in northwestern France and Belgium, 1940–45.

Broken Eagles I: FW 190 D. Pictorial series of the Luftwaffe.

"Camouflage and Markings of the Luftwaffe." *Aircraft* 1.

Cooper, Matthew. *The German Air Force, 1933–45.* London: Jane's, 1981. Good bibliography.

Davies, Brian C. *Luftwaffe Air Crews—Battle of Britain 1940.* London: Arms and Armour Press, 1974. Key Uniform Guides 4 Series.

Fleming, P. *Invasion 1940.* London: Hart Davies, 1957. Published in the United States as *Operation Sea Lion* (New York: Simon and Schuster, 1956). Account of the German preparation for the invasion of Britain.

Galland, Adolf. *The First and the Last.* London: Methuen, 1955 (English edition); Fontana/Collins, 1970.

Gehm, Harry. "German Fighter Pilot's Daring Exploit over England." *Berliner Zeitung,* 4 September 1940.

Green, W. *The Augsburg Eagle.* Messerschmitt Bf 109.

Grinsell, Robert. *Messerschmitt Bf 109.* London: Jane's, 1980.

Hamilton, James Douglas. *Motive for a Mission.* Edinburgh: Mainstream Publishing, 1974.

Hess, Wolf Rudiger. *My Father, Rudolf Hess.* London: W. H. Allen, 1968. See also PRO Hess AIR 19/546, INF 1/912, WO 199/3288A.

Ishoven, Armand van. *The Luftwaffe in the Battle of Britain.* London: Ian Allan, 1980.

Kosin, Rudiger. *The German Fighter since 1915.* London: Putnam, 1988.

Murray, Williamson. *Strategy for Defeat, 1933–45.* London: Grafton Books, Collins Group, 1988.

Philpott, B. *Fighters Defending the Reich. Photo Album* (magasine). Photos from German sources.

Price, Alfred. *Instruments of Darkness.* William Kimber. London: William Kimber.

———. *Pictorial History of the Luftwaffe.* London: Ian Allan, 1965.

———. "Luftwaffe." In *Purnell's History of the Second World War,* no. 10. London: Macdonald, 1989. With an introduction by the German ace Generalleutenant Adolf Galland.

Rudel, Hans Ulrich. *Stuka Pilot.* London: Euphoria Books and Transworld Publishers.

Rutherford, Ward. *Blitzkreig 1940.* London: Bison Books, 1979.

Schneekluth, Frank. *Die Ersten und Die Letzen.* German edition, 1953. See Galland entry.

Stark, Rudolf. *Wings of War.* A German airman's diary of the last year of WW1.

Tolliver, R. *The Blond Knight of Germany.* London: Barker, 1970.

Wakefield, Kenneth. *Luftwaffe Encore.* London: William Kimber, 1979. A study of two attacks in September 1940.

Wentzel, Fritz. *Single or Return?* London: William Kimber.

GHOSTS

All RAF stations hold memories of the past, especially those which are now untenanted. Some are known to have ghosts which have been both seen and heard, such as that at Lindholme, now an open prison, or at Waltham and Leeming, or that which was exorcised on TV in 1989. Of the Fighter Station ghosts there are several at West Malling and Croydon, both Battle of Britain stations. Worth looking at as basic sources for research are the following:

Forsyth, Frederick. *The Shepherd.* London: Hutchinson, 1975. Fiction, but concerns experiences encountered by other pilots. Evocative and written by a master. The 1976 Corgi edition is well illustrated by Lou Feck. The Hutchinson 1975 is illustrated by Chris Foss. The story is of a Vampire a/c of 1956 and a Mosquito of 1943. Neither of the Battle of Britain period, but useful.

Halpenny, Bruce Barrymore. *Ghost Stations.* Devon: Merlin Books, 1986. Contains poetry and Battle of Britain stories about North Weald, Boscombe Down, Upavon, Hawkinge and many others. No bibliography or index, but good verifiable dates, names and locations.

McKee, Alexander. *Into the Blue*. London: Souvenir Press, 1981. Subtitled "Great Mysteries of Aviation," it covers a wide period of time. Well researched personal recollections. No bibliography, but good chapter references. The 1940 bombing of Portsmouth connects with the Battle of Britain. This latter can be checked in ADM 477 at the PRO, 22 December 1940.

UFOs are another phenomenon altogether and not to be confused with the above, but for those interested there is a reference to Topcliffe, in Yorkshire, in AIR 20. It has nothing to do with the Battle of Britain.

GLOSTER GLADIATORS

When the war started several squadrons still had biplanes—Gladiators—but only 247 Squadron flew them during the Battle. There were not enough monoplane types to re-equip any but those in the front line. Roborough, which is now Plymouth Airport, was too small to accommodate Spitfires and Hurricanes, so 247, brought down from the Shetlands to defend the naval dockyards there, retained its biplanes. A great deal has been written about this aircraft, but not much about its role in the Battle. For this, see 247's operations books in AIR 27. See also the following:

Air Enthusiast (March 1973), p. 134.

Bowyer, M.J.F. *Fighting Colours*. London: 1969. pp. 27, 47.

Green, William. *Famous Fighters of World War 2*, vol 2. London: Macdonald, 1957.

Maclure, V. *Gladiators over Norway*. Blackwood's Magasine (February-March 1941).

Mason, Francis K. *The Gloster Gladiator*. Macdonald Aircraft Monograph, 1964; Windsor, Berks: Profile Publications, Aircraft in Profile 98, 1965.

Price, Alfred. *The Hardest Day: 18 August 1940*. London and New York: Arms and Armour Press, 1979, 1988. Very good detail of witnesses, bibliography, rank equivalents RAF/Luftwaffe, units and strengths of both, maps, losses, etc.

Terraine, John. *The Right of the Line*. London: Hodder and Stoughton, 1985; Sceptre, 1988. Very good bibliography and index.

Gladiators entered service with the RAF and FAA (Fleet Air Arm) and were the last of the biplane fighters. For descriptive details see:

Weale and Barker. *Combat Aircraft of World War II*. London: Arms and Armour Press, 1977; Bracken Books, 1985).

THE GUINEA PIG CLUB

There are many associations which gather together those who fought in the Battle of Britain, either as flyers or on the ground. Examples include the Goldfish Club, the Caterpillar Club (for those who bailed out or came down "in the drink''), the Battle of Britain Association, and many more. Probably the most moving of them all is The Guinea Pig Club.

There are many references to the club in the books by those pilots who were badly burned when they crashed in flames—Geoffrey Page and Richard Hillary, to name only two. Their hands, legs, and faces often had to be totally restructured and many bear the scars still, but at least they are able to live a relatively normal life again. There are people from later wars, such as the Falklands and the Gulf, who have benefitted from what was learned on these early guinea pigs, who acted as pioneers of these new kinds of surgical procedures.

Sir Archibald McIndoe was the famous surgeon on whom they all depended; his successful experimental hospital was located in East Grinstead. See Peter Williams and Ted Harrison, *McIndoe's Army* (London: Pelham, 1979); this book has a full list of Guinea Pigs and an account of the surgery and Club formed by these patients. There is also a short bibliography of books written by Guniea Pigs, one of the most well known living today is Geoffrey Page. The Thames Television documentary film ''The Guinea Pigs'' was based on this book: Edward Bishop, *The Guinea Pig Club* (London: Macmillan, 1963).

HURRICANES

Allward, Maurice. *Hurricane Special.* London: Ian Allan, 1975.

Bishop, Edward. *The Guinea Pig Club* (London: Macmillan, 1963).

———. *Hurricane.* Shrewsbury: Airlife, 1986. Good subject bibliography.

Bowyer, Chaz. *Hurricane at War.* London: Ian Allan, 1975.

Clarke, R. M, comp. *The Hawker Hurricane Portfolio.* London: Business Press International, 1986. Articles from contemporary issues of *Aeroplane Monthly.* Brooklands Aircraft Portfolio.

Cooksley, Peter. *Battle of Britain.* London: Osprey, 1986. Aircam Aviation Series Sl. Hurricane, Spitfire, Messerschmitt.

Emory, John. *Source Book of World War II Aircraft.* Poole Dorset: Blandford Press.

Fozard, John W., ed. *Sydney Camm and the Hurricane: Master Fighter Designer and His Finest Achievement.* Shrewsbury: Airlife.

Franks, Norman. *Hurricane at War 2.* London: Ian Allan, 1986.

Gallico, Paul. *The Hurricane Story.* London: Michael Joseph, 1959. Well illustrated with Battle of Britain personalities.

Hawker Hurricane Described. Victoria, Australia: Kookaburra Technical Publications, 1970.

Hawker Hurricane 1. London: Profile Publications, 1962.

Hurricane, Clouded by Legend. Kingston-upon-Thames: British Aerospace, 1990.

Jackson, Robert. *Hawker Hurricane.* London: Blandford Press, 1988. Well illustrated and with squadron histories.

James, Derek N. *Hawker: An Aircraft Album.* London: Ian Allan, 1972.

Kelly, Terence. *Hurricane and Spitfire Pilots at War.* London: William Kimber, 1986.

Lloyd, F.H.M. *Hurricane: The Story of a Great Fighter.* Harborough Publishing, 1945.

Mackenzie, Wg Cdr. *Hurricane Combat: Nine Lives of a Fighter Pilot.* London: William

Kimber, 1988. 501 and 247 Squadrons, and POW. Very well documented. Proceeds to the RAF Benevolent Fund.
Mason, Francis K. *Hawker Aircraft since 1920*. London: Putnam, 1961. Has production and service detail for identification.
———. *Hawker Hurricane*. Bourne End: Aston, 1962.
———. *Hawker Hurricane*. London: Macdonald, 1962.
Robertson, Bruce, and Gerald Scarborough. *Classic Aircraft, Their History and How to Model Them*. Patrick Stephens/Airfix Ltd. Series, 1974.
Stewart, Adrian. *Hurricane*. London: William Kimber, 1982.

See also BIOGRAPHIES: AIRCRAFT; and COLLECTIONS.

As the Battle of Britain started, Italy declared war on Britain and France, 11 June 1940. Although not part of the fight for Britain between the RAF and the Luftwaffe, many Hurricanes played their part in the defence and siege of Malta. See Christopher Shores and Brian Cull, *Malta: the Hurricane Years*.

There are Hurricanes at the following locations (serial number correct at time of writing):

Type	Location	Serial Number
MkI	Science Museum, South Kensington, London	L1592
	BoB Hanger, RAF Museum Hendon	P2617 and P3175
	Shuttleworth Collection	Z7015
MkII	RAF's Battle of Britain Memorial Flight at RAF Coningsby	LF363
		LF738
		LF751
		PZ865
	B. S. Grey, owner, Coventry	G-Huri
MkIV	Museum of Science & Industry, Birmingham	KX289
	D. W. Arnold, owner, Blackbushe	——
	R. Lamplough, Duxford	——
Replicas	Torbay Aircraft Museum, Higher Blagdon	
	J. Berkeley, owner, N. Weald	
	Hawkinge Aeronautical Trust	BAPC-64
	T. J. Loakes, owner	BAPC-68

As originals are being moved rapidly into safer keeping and being replaced by replicas, please check all these before visiting. This is also advisable in regard to Gate Guardians at RAF airfields. In some cases visiting is only by appointment apart from public museums, for all types of aircraft. Those on RAF stations, for example the Hurricanes on the Battle of Britain Memorial Flight (BBMF), may be seen on the station's annual Open Day. Check also with Mason's *Hawker Hurricane* and with the various museum guides.

Spitfires are found at the following locations:

Type	Location	Serial Number
300	RAF Museum, Hendon	K9942

1A	Science Museum, South Kensington, London	P9444
	Imperial War Museum, Lambeth, London	R6915
	Battle of Britain Museum, Hendon	X4590
	The Hon P. Lindsay, owner, Booker	AR213
321	Battle of Britain Memorial Flight, RAF Coningsby	P7350
11A	Dumfries & Galloway AG, Tinwald Downs	P7540
349V	Battle of Britain Memorial Flight, RAF Coningsby	AB910
	Shuttleworth Trust at Old Warden	AR501
	RAF Museum, Manchester A & SM	BL614
	RAF Linton on Ouse	BM597
	RAF Wattisham	EP120
359 HFV111	R Lamplugh, Bristol	MV154

A replica from the film *Piece of Cake* is located at the D-Day Museum, Shoreham, West Sussex. See also the Spitfire Society Collection, Hall of Aviation, Albert Road South, Southampton S01 1FR.

The same checks as for Hurricanes should be made before quoting or visiting, and also with Morgan and Shacklady's *Spitfire: The History.*

INTELLIGENCE, EVIDENCE AND OBSERVATION

Babington-Smith, Constance. *Evidence in Camera.* London: Chatto and Windus, 1974. Photo intelligence in WW2; author discovered flying bomb sites at Penemunde.

Barker, Ralph. *Aviator Extraordinary: The Sidney Cotton Story.* 1969. Photo reconnaissance detail.

Brome, Vincent. *The Way Back.* London: Cassel, 1957. See also article in *Observer,* 27 October 1974. Story of Lt Commander Pat O'Leary, GC DSO RN, and Flt Lt Taffy Higginson, DFM, escape line organisers.

Clayton, Aileen. *The Enemy Is Listening.* London: Hutchinson, 1980. Story of the Y Service and the WAAFs involved. Author was the first WAAF to be commissioned as Intelligence Officer; was then named A. B. Morris. Good bibliography, index and diagrams.

Foot, M. R. *SOE, the Special Operations Executive, 1940–45.* London: BBC 1984. In memory of Ronald Lewin.

Hinsley, F. M. *British Intelligence in the Second World War.* Vol. 1. London: HMSO, 4 vols. On open shelves at PRO. Has details of proposed invasion of Britain, Operation Sea Lion, 17/18 October, and Moonlight Sonata (raid on Coventry 14 November 1940).

Johnson, Brian. *The Secret War.* London: BBC, 1978.

Jones, R. V. *Most Secret War.* London: Hamish Hamilton, 1978.

Lewin, Ronald. *Ultra Goes to War.* London: Hutchinson, 1978. Good chapter notes, bibliography and index.

Mead, Peter. *The Eye in the Sky.* London: HMSO, Air observation 1785–1945. Good bibliography.

Stevenson, William. *A Man Called Intrepid: The Secret War 1939–45.* London: Macmillan, 1976; London: Sphere Books, 1977. The author is no relative of the subject Sir William Stevenson. The subject was a WW1 air Ace. Good date list, index and reference in text.

West, Nigel. *M16*. London: Weidenfeld and Nicolson, 1983. British Secret Intelligence Service Ops, 1909–45. No bibliography but good index and appendix.

Winterbotham, F. W. *Secret and Personal*. London: William Kimber, 1969.

———. *The Ultra Secret*. London: Weidenfeld and Nicolson, 1974.

———. *The Ultra Spy*. London: Macmillan, 1989.

Young, Gordon. *In Trust and Treason*. London: Studio Vista, 1959. Tells of Suzanne Warenghem, married to Paul Cole.

Many of these books contain comprehensive bibliographies on these and related subjects. For further information on Photo Reconnaissance, see under this title at PRO in files AIR 41/6 and in a monograph in ADM 233/54.

JOURNALS, EXCERPTS FROM

Boorman, H. R. Pratt. *Hell's Corner, 1940*. Maidstone: Kent Messenger, 1942. The *Kent Messenger* is the local newspaper covering the extreme southeast of England, the area which saw most of the battle for London in the Battle of Britain. It covers the county for these and other months and is available at the Newspaper Library, Colindale, Hendon, North London. See also Blaise Line at British Library.

Hayson, G.D.L. "How the Few Saved the Many." *Wings* 9, no. 10 (September 1950).

"Hitler's Battle of Britain Plan." *RAF Flying Review* 15, no. 2.

Joubert, Air Chief Marshal Philip. "How the Way Was Paved for the Battle of Britain." *RAF Flying Review* 5, no. 2 (1949).

Slessor, J. C. "Looking Back on the Battle of Britain." *The Listener* (magasine of BBC Radio), 19 September 1957.

von Plehove, Friederich-Karl. "Operation Sea Lion 1940." *RUSI Journal* (March 1973).

Microfilms of newspapers (including the *Kent Messenger*, which covered the county of Kent) and journals are for sale at the British Newspaper Library, Colindale. A list is available from the British Library, London NW9 5HE. See also BLAISE-LINE in BIBLIOGRAPHIES section and MAGASINES AND JOURNALS section.

LIBRARIES

British Library, British Museum, Gt Russell Street, Bloomsbury, London WC1. The main copyright library; this has copies of every book published in the UK. The catalogue lists under subject and author. None may be borrowed, and a reader's ticket is required. Copyright libraries in the other parts of the UK hold similar collections.

Fawcett Library of Women's History, City of London Polytechnic, Old Castle Street, London EI 7 NT. For women's role in the RAF, in plotting and control, in Anti-Aircraft and Cypher duties, as well as the WAAF in general.

Greater London Record Office, 40 Northampton Road, London EC1. Research facilities for London's history.

Guildhall Library, Aldermanbury, London EC2. Research facilities for history of the City of London.

Imperial War Museum, Lambeth, London SE1. Here is held a full index of the Commonwealth War Graves Commission's lists.

London Library, 14 St. James Square SW1.

Newspaper Library, a branch of the British Library, at Colindale, in the same road as the RAF Museum, London NW 9. Described in NEWSPAPERS section.

RAF Museum, Hendon. Has a comprehensive library of books and journals relating to its subject.

Society of Genealogists, 14 Charterhouse Bdgs, Goswell Road, London EC1M 7BA.

Most local libraries allow temporary reader's tickets for borrowing; many have a good reference section. Those in the area concerned are the most likely to hold a collection pertaining to their own district and interests. See also PICTURE LIBRARIES section.

MAGASINES AND JOURNALS

After the Battle. Battle of Britain Prints International, 3 New Plaistow Road, Stratford, London E15 3JA.

Air Mail. Journal of the Royal Air Force Association, 43 Grove Park, London W4 3RX.

Flight Magazine. Quadrant House, Sutton, Surrey. During the war years, published casualty lists. Has own library, or may be seen at British Library's Newspaper Library, Colindale. Also at Quadrant House may be found *Kelly's Directories* for the whole country, a full run.

Fly Past. Key Publications Ltd., P.O Box 100, Stamford, Lincs PE9 lXQ.

Images of War. Marshall Cavendish Partworks, 58 Old Compton St., London WlV 5PA, in association with the Imperial War Museum. A three-part fortnightly pack, first appeared 1988. Part 2, The Battle of Britain. Contains a War Diary of events.

Journal of the Royal Air Force. M o D.

Proceedings of the Royal Air Force Historical Society.

Royal Air Force News. Turnstile House, 98 High Holborn, London WClV 6LL.

War in the Air. Room 214, Prospect House, 9–13 Ewell Rd., Cheam, Surrey SMl 4QQ, in association with *Flight* and *Aeroplane Monthly*, by Prospect Magasines. This magasine is unusual in that it consists of contemporary reprints from *Aeroplane* and *Flight*, dating from September 1938, No. 1 appeared June 1989.

World War Two Investigator. 68 Staines Rd., Hounslow, Mdx TW3 3LF. Monthly from May 1988.

Picture Post, *Tit Bits*, *Reveille*, and *Blighty* are contemporary magasines and can be seen along with others similar at the British Library, or at the Newspaper Library, its branch at Colindale, North London. A reader's ticket is required.

Newspapers of 1989 and 1990 will contain many 50th anniversary articles about the outbreak of war in 1939 and the Battle of Britain. Local papers will have articles about their area, e.g., *The Evening Herald*, Plymouth, 2 September 1989.

The following magasines/journals are without addresses and are available at the Newspaper Library at Colindale, Hendon, north London: *Aeroplane, Pilot, Profile*, and *RAF News*.

MEMORIALS

Biggin Hill: The RAF Station is now closed, but the memorial chapel may be visited by prior permission of the guardroom.

St Clement Dane Church: Central Church of the RAF, Strand, London. Originally ninth century. Sir Christopher Wren's design destroyed in 1941, fully restored and rededicated in 1958. Holds RAF memorials and squadron badges.

Eagle Squadron Memorial: Grosvenor Square, London.

Memorial to the Royal Norwegian Air Force at North Weald. For detail, see *The Battle of Britain, Then and Now*, Winston S. Ramsey, ed.

The Polish Memorial at Ruislip, Middlesex, and the Polish Memorial at Newark.

War Graves Commission. Commonwealth. Photographs and lists including Runnymede, where are commemorated those with no known graves.

Westminster Abbey: The Battle of Britain window, dedicated 1947. Designed by Hugh Easton.

To all these may be added the Roll of Honour which many existing squadrons retain of their past members. Information about this may be obtained from the various air museums and archives. A few are held at the PRO; more may be obtained via the Air Crew Association, Fighter Pilots' Association and similar organisations. Some are retained in the churches nearest to a base on which the squadron served; for example, in 1989 the Roll of Honour for 247 Squadron was lodged at a memorial service at the parish church of High Ercall in Shropshire, and its full version was dedicated there in 1990, their 50th year. Some Battle of Britain names are remembered on it. Another example is that in the church at St Eval, Cornwall, for all squadrons which served there.

Please remember that *all* wreckage, no matter how remote or well documented, is now a protected site. Permission must be sought from the Home Office and the local Aviation Society to investigate. If there is the smallest chance that there may still be human remains, as has often been the case, these rules *must* be strictly observed, as such sites are classified as memorials and war graves and *must not* be disturbed. If such are found, permission must also be sought from the next of kin.

Many airfields carry their own memorials, often recently erected by local enthusiasts or Squadron Associations.

Books and Lists for Further Reading

Imperial War Museum, London. Data bank of War Memorials Project. For example see the Barclay Memorial at Cromer Parish Church, Norfolk, in honor of Richard George Arthur Barclay, DFC, Battle of Britain pilot shot down and escaped from France, fell at El Alemein 17 July 1942.

"Memorials in Essex." *Fly Past* (August 1989).

Middlebrook, Martin, and Chris Everitt. *Bomber Command War Diaries.* London: Viking, 1985; London: Penguin, 1985. Photographs of cemeteries.

Smith, David J. *Britain's Military Airfields.* Wellingborough: Patrick Stephens, 1989. Contains a list of memorials.

St Catherine's House, Office of the General Registrar (GRO). List of RAF War Dead (index).

Their Name Liveth. London: Methuen, 1955. Photographs of War Graves Cemeteries 1914–18 and 1939–45 for the War Graves Commission.

MUSEUMS

Directories of museums are constantly being updated. It is therefore advisable to check with the latest editions before visiting. A few museums are permanent, such as the following:

D-Day Museum at Shoreham, West Sussex. Outside stands one of the replica Spitfires used in the film *Piece of Cake.* On the A27 route.

Fleet Air Arm Museum, RNAS Yeovilton, Ilchester, Somerset, on the A303.

Imperial War Museum, Lambeth, London, and its aircraft detachment at Duxford, south of Cambridge on the A505.

Military Aviation Museum at Tangmere, near Chichester, West Sussex. Original aircraft stand outside. On the A27 route.

RAF Museum, Hendon. Series of several publications: Lists of Subjects, Research Aids, Periodical Catalogue. Has a good shop and archival department. Appointment needed for the latter. Has a Battle of Britain hangar.

Science Museum, South Kensington, London, and Wroughton, Swindon.

A few other sites are:

Battle of Britain Museum, Hawkinge, Kent.

Battle of Britain Museum in the RAF Museum, Hendon.

Battle of Britain Memorial Flight, RAF Coningsby, Lincolnshire.

Duxford, Imperial War Museum, Duxford airfield, Cambridge CB2 4QR.

Hall of Aviation, Southampton SO1 1FR. The Spitfire Society is based here.

North Weald, Battle of Britain airfield, Blake Hall, Ongar, Essex.

RAF Cosford, near Wolverhampton.

Spitfire Memorial Building at Manston, Ramsgate, Kent, which has the Spitfire LF XVl used in the film *Reach for the Sky*.

Shoreham Aircraft Museum, Shoreham Village, Sevenoaks, Kent.

Wroughton, Science Museum Air Extension, Swindon, SN4 9NS.

Many former and present RAF Stations have "gate guardians"; these are representative of the aircraft which served there. They were, until recently, the originals, but owing to the necessity of conservation most of these are now faithful replicas. Other representative aircraft may be found in non-RAF museums such as the Museum of Army Flying, Middle Wallop, Hampshire, southwest of Andover, and the War Museum, Durford Hill, Warnham, nr Horsham, Sussex.

Others may have changed or been amalgamated; check before visiting. For countrywide comprehensive lists which include location and times of opening, see the following titles (check first, as they are updated regularly):

British Aviation Museums and Collections. Stamford, Lincs: Key Publishing.

British Aircraft Museums Directory. Bourne End, Bucks: Aston Publications.

Vintage Aircraft Directory.

MUSIC

Music, mainly popular songs, was very important; songs kept up the morale of the people on the ground and singing was an essential part of camp life for those in the Services. The cheerful gaiety of many songs was encouraged, and as soon as the tide began to turn it was reflected in the forward-looking words. More serious music like "Spitfire Prelude" gained popularity after the danger was passed.

Popular Songs, Artists of

Al Bowly: Popular singer who was killed in the Blitz at the Cafe de Paris, Leicester Square 1941.

Max Bygraves: "Sing-along Wartime Songs," 1989. Popular present-day singer who was in the RAF. Audiotapes and videos.

Vera Lynn: the "Forces Sweetheart," and author of her autobiography. See author section. Some of her songs include "Wish Me Luck as You Wave Me Goodbye," (also sung by Gracie Fields), "Yours," "White Cliffs of Dover," "We'll Meet Again," "There'll Always Be an England."

Anne Shelton: Popular wartime singer and pin-up girl.

Composers

Richard Addinsell: "The Warsaw Concerto," for the film *Dangerous Moonlight* starring Anton Walbrook.

Walford Davies: "The RAF March Past," recorded by the Central Band of the Royal Air Force.

Leighton Lucas: Composer and BBC conductor who wrote the incidental music for the film *Target for Tonight*. Served three years in the RAF.

William Walton: Composer of serious wartime music, particularly "The Battle of Britain Suite" for film *The Battle of Britain*, United Artists 1969. Also "Spitfire Prelude and Fugue," recorded by EMI.

Publications

Melody Maker: Newspaper of the music trade in London. Back numbers available at the Newspaper Library, Colindale, Hendon, north London. Includes lists songs, music of all types issued for 1940. Miscellaneous song titles, such as "Lily Marlene" (popular song on both sides of the Battle), "If I Only Had Wings," "Our Soldiers, Our Sailors and Our Airmen," "He Wears a Pair of Silver Wings," "When the Lights Go On Again," and many more will be listed here in detail.

"Nostalgia Street." Radio program on LBC, London's local radio station, by Sandy Forbes from his own collection, 1986. A great many songs from the 1940s.

World War II Songs. London: Wise Publications, Music Sales Ltd., 1990. Also has pictures, text and commentary on the Home Front.

NAVY AND FLEET AIR ARM PART IN THE BATTLE

The Channel and Atlantic convoys had, of course, to be kept going, the more so after the Fall of France. The main responsibility at sea for this, apart from air cover, belonged to the navy. References to these dates can be found in the ADM class lists of the PRO and the many books published on the subject. A good general reference to the Fleet Air Arm can be found in *The Fleet Air Arm*, prepared for the Admiralty (London: HMSO, 1943). Aside from the two FAA squadrons involved and listed earlier, this is a good account of the training involved and of those pilots loaned to and trained by the RAF. Three of these pilots were sent to a front line Hurricane squadron, reformed and commanded by Sqn Ldr Douglas Bader, which had just returned from France, and were now in East Anglia. Others were trained with the RAF at such OTUs at Hawarden, North Wales.

For the protection of the Merchant Fleet, some merchant ships were fitted with catapult Hurricanes to be launched from their decks in convoy, but these were not fully introduced until a year later. Look among some RAF squadron records for the volunteers to the Merchant Service Fighter Units (MSFUs).

FAA pilots, seconded to Coastal Command during this period and in the Fleet Requirement units, may also be found in the relevant PRO files. Many FAA detachments were "lodger" units on RAF airfields. Look for these in AIR 27 and in ADM class records at the PRO. See also:

Sturtivant, Ray. *Squadrons of the Fleet Air Arm*. Saffron Walden: Air Britain, 1984. On open shelves at the PRO. Full details by number, place, date and equipment. 804 Squadron (Sea Gladiators) and 808 (Fulmars) were the two FAA squadrons involved in the Battle of Britain. See AIR 27.

For more information on the FAA's part in the Battle and in these two squadrons in particular, see also the FAA Museum, its library and archive, at RNAS Yeovilton.

NEWSPAPERS

Every newspaper of the time carried Battle of Britain news, successes and defeats; some had casualty lists and named losses. But those around London were the ones likely to carry most detail. These can be found, both daily and weekly editions, at the Newspaper Library at Colindale, which is part of the British Library.

There is a booklet list of those papers for which there are microfilms for sale at the library containing London local newspapers with comprehensive dates; London nationals; the remaining UK, local and national; Allied, Commonwealth and Foreign newspapers; and English provincials.

For example, Kent was the most over-flown county, and the area between Margate and London was colloquially known as "Bomb Alley." There are four newspapers covering this county, with several from an earlier and later period giving a historical background. Some of them include Sussex also.

If looking for a particular airman, pilot or ground staff member whose home town is known, it is probable there will be an account in the local paper; it is likely this newspaper will be at Colindale.

From the *Daily Telegraph*, there is a series of cuttings in scrapbook form at the Society of Genealogists, London, covering several years of the paper's publication. The war years 1939–45 are of particular research value for the period of the Battle. Births, marriages and deaths as well as Missing and In Memoriam are included. For the latter look further on than 1940 exclusively.

Many other national and local newspapers give similar information. *Writers and Artists Year Book* for the war period also gives titles and addresses of local and national papers and journals, as does *Writers Handbook*, ed. Barry Turner (London: Macmillan, 1992.)

The 50th anniversary of the outbreak of war on 3 September 1939 was recorded in special supplements of many newspapers during the month of September 1989. The 50th anniversary of the Battle of Britain is similarly recorded, and indeed was on many previous anniversaries. It is possible, therefore, that if the original issue cannot be found, the anniversary issue may be located.

NEW ZEALAND

Fairclough, N. W. *New Zealanders in the Battle of Britain*. Wellington, N.Z.: War History Branch, Department of Internal Affairs, 1950.

Houlton, Johnnie. *Spitfire Strikes*. London: John Murray, 1985. Pilot's story of an NZ fighter.

Hunt, Leslie. *Defence until Dawn*. Privately printed, 1949. 488 Sq RNZAF.

Kay, Air Vice Marshal C. E. *The Restless Sky*. London: Harrap, 1964. Former Air Chief of Staff New Zealand. Autobiography of an airman.

Midland Counties Publications. *To the Four Winds: 40 Sqn RNZAF*. Earl Shilton: Midland Counties Publications. Though this is a transport squadron formed in 1943, there is background history to New Zealanders in battle.

Mitchell, A. W. *New Zealanders in the Air War*. London: Harrap, 1945.

Orange, Vincent. *The Road to Biggin Hill*. Shrewsbury: Airlife, 1986. About Wg Cdr Johnny Checketts, DSO DFC NZ.

———. *Sir Keith Park*. London: Methuen, 1984.

Sanders, James. *The Time of My Life*. NZ: Minerva Ltd., 1967.

———. *Venturer Courageous*. NZ: Hutchinson, 1983.

Thompson, H. L. *New Zealanders with the RAF*. 3 vols. Wellington, N.Z.: War History Branch, Department of National Affairs, 1959; Vol. 1, European Theatre, September 1939–December 1942; Vol. 2, European Theatre, January 1943–May 1945; vol. 3, Medium and Middle East, Southeast Asia.

War History Branch. *RNZAF: The Official History*. 3 vols. Wellington, N.Z.: War History Branch, Department of National Affairs, 1953.

75 Squadron, formed in 1939 with Wellingtons, had a New Zealand Flight at Feltwell, which began operations soon after formation.

See also James Edgar "Cobber" Kain who was a famous New Zealand Air Ace in the Battle of Britain and in 1 and 73 Squadrons. He is mentioned in, and the book is dedicated to him, Noel Monks, *Squadrons Up!* Also refer to PRO AIR 27.

PHOTO COLLECTIONS

Many collections of photographs are in private hands but may be loaned on payment of a copyright and reproduction fee. Others are the property and copyright of the magasine in which they appeared, such as *Fly Past*, *Air Mail*, and *RAF News*. All should be approached directly. In the case of an author, via the publisher, copyright will still apply. Some, such as the War Collection of Cecil Beaton, are at the Imperial War Museum and were published by them with Jane's Publishers in 1981. The Imperial War Museum is at Lambeth, London.

There are also collections at the Museum of Military Aviation, Tangmere, Chichester, West Sussex; and at the RAF Museum, Hendon, in north London. The back pages of the magasines listed above have addresses of other collections.

The Public Record Office at Kew holds an index of all photographs found in the documents in its protection. It carries an AIR class reference to the relevant text about sites, buildings, aircraft, and personnel. Bromides may be ordered from these. Photographs may also be ordered from documents at the Colindale Newspaper Library. This archive is part of the British Library.

Barry Turner's *The Writer's Handbook* has lists of other picture libraries, such as Mary Evans Picture Library, Blackheath, London.

For Chaz Bowyer's Photo Collection, contact the publisher. The Ken Woolley Photo Collection may be found at Berkswell, Coventry. See also local County Record Offices and Reference Libraries which carry photographs referring to the Battle of Britain area in the south and southeast of England.

For the most part, these are collections of photographs. Picture Libraries (see next section) carry many different kinds of pictures, artists' drawings, portraits, newspaper and magasine cuttings, as well as historical references.

PICTURE LIBRARIES

Yellow Pages, the commercial telephone directory, has a list of Picture Libraries from which photographs and other pictures are on loan for a fee. A few of these include: Aspect Picture Library; Mary Evans Picture Library, 59 Tranquil Vale Blackheath, London SE3 OBS; and others including addresses of additional research facilities. The material will be divided into categories such as "the Battle of Britain" and are chargeable by time and purpose. The *Illustrated London News* also rents out copies of pictures found in its pages.

Other library and research agencies are listed in Barry Turner's *The Writer's Handbook*, which lists all similar places where research may be done, help sought, facilities available, times of opening, and so on. Copyright and reproduction fees apply to most other photograph sources including newspapers and news agencies.

Aviation journalists and publishers who may have private picture libraries are listed in *Flight International Directory* (United Kingdom), compiled and edited by Malcolm Ginsberg and published annually by Flight International, Potters Bar, Herts.

Tourist Offices often have pictures of their areas for loan. Generally there is no charge, though proper credit acknowledgment is requested.

PILOTS' LOG BOOKS

Pilots' log books are found at the PRO in AIR/4. There are a great many log books to choose from, but the list is by no means complete, as those left unclaimed a few years after the war ended were destroyed. The rest remain in the owners' hands or in those of the family; a few are at the RAF Museum at Hendon, whilst some still turn up in secondhand booksellers' catalogues.

A few listed as having Battle of Britain references are selected here from the PRO's AIR index:

AIR 4/8 P/O P.A. Burnell-Phillips of 607 Squadron

AIR 4/11 Sqn Ldr G. P. Christie

AIR 4/17 F/O J. H. Coghlan

AIR 4/19 Wg W. E. Coope

AIR 4/20 P/O J. L. Crispe

AIR 4/21 Flt Lt D. M. Crooke, DFC

AIR 4/32 Wg Cdr A. Eyre

AIR 4/58 Sqn Ldr B.J.E. Lane

AIR 4/77 P/O W. L. McKnight, DFC

There are others who were not pilots, but miscellaneous aircrew, and logs of other ranks which might offer personal and immediate background. Those lodged with the PRO are there as donations by the family after the owner's death, or by the owner himself.

Cross reference these with the operations books of the squadrons mentioned and the corresponding Combat Reports. Officers' service numbers may be checked in the Air Force List, on the open shelves at the PRO. Paddy Finucane's log book is a photocopy of the original, which is held by his family. See the biography by Doug Stokes, which has a useful acknowledgment list.

PLACES

Bond, S. J. *RAF St Athan, 1938–88.* 19 & 32 Sq Mustangs, 4 Squadons of Typhoon and Tempests, and RAF Hospital. Aircraft post–Battle of Britain, but good background to the period.

Burgess, Pat, and Andy Saunders. *Battle over Sussex, 1940.* Midhurst: Middleton Press, 1990.

Copeman, Geoff. *Silksheen: History of East Kirkby.* 57 and 630 Sqn RAF bombers, and USAAF.

Dodsworth, Ted. *Wings over Yorkshire.* Pioneer aviation, 1909–52.

James, Ian. *The Defenders of Bristol.* Use of decoy sites in WW2.

———. *History of RAF Lulsgate Bottom.* WW2 flying training school, now Bristol Airport.

Kinsey, Gordon. *Martlesham Heath.* Sudbury, Suffolk: Terence Dalton, 1975.

Lunn, Brian, and Gavin Harland, comp. *Aircraft Down: Air Crashes around Wetherby, Yorkshire, 1939–1945.* Pontefract, Yorkshire: Hardwick, 1985. Although about bombers and not specifically about the Battle of Britain, these two books give good coverage and have good bibliographies and guidelines. Other research groups produce similar.

———. *Aircraft Down II: Air Crashes in Wharfedale and Nidderdale.* Pontefract, Yorkshire: Hardwick Publications, 1985.

Ogden, Bob. *Biggin on the Bump.* Froglets Pub., 1990.

Shapland, Jean. *The Memories Linger On.* Trevisker Farm, St Eval, Cornwall: Privately printed, 1989. A collection of Reminiscences of Wartime St Eval.

Teague, Dennis C. *Roborough-Plymouth City Airport, 1929–1989.* Plymouth, 1990.

Thampson, R. J. *Battle over Essex.* Chelmsford: Clarke, 1946.
Wall, Robert. *From Boxkite to Concorde: Bristol's Civil and Military Aircraft.*

Though fighter pilots took the greater part, it was not only they who fought the Battle of Britain. Bomber squadrons made daily operational raids on Germany, dropping both bombs and leaflets. To find the squadrons which took part in these vital months, and the bases from where they took off, see:

Middlebrook, Martin, and Chris Everitt. *The Bomber Command War Diaries.* London and New York: Viking/Penguin, 1985. An invaluable operational reference book covering 1939–1945, with copious detail on squadrons and missions.

POETRY

High Flight

Oh, I have slipped the surly bonds of earth
And danced the skies on laughter-silvered wings;
Sunward I've climbed, and joined the tumbling mirth
Of sun-split clouds—and done a hundred things.
You have not dreamed of—wheeled and soared and swung
High in the sunlit silence, Hov'ring there,
I've chased the shouting wind along, and flung
My eager craft through footless halls of air.
Up, up the long delirious, burning blue
I've topped the windswept heights with easy grace
Where never lark, nor even eagle flew.
And, while with silent, lifting mind I've trod
The high untrespassed sanctity of space,
Put out my hand, and touched the face of God.

Pilot Officer John Gillespie Magee, RCAF, aged 19, was killed on active service and buried near RAF Digby, December 1941, in Scopwick churchyard. This work was quoted by President Ronald Reagan after the U.S. space disaster, Challenger in 1982. This poem first appeared in *More Poems from The Forces* (1943).

See also AMERICANS section.

Balfour of Inchrye, Lord. *Biggin Hill and Other Poems.* Served in RAF and RFC and was Parliamentary Under Secretary of State for Air 1938–45.
Dixon, Ronald, ed. *Echoes in the Sky.* Dorset: Blandford Press, 1982. An anthology of aviation verse from two world wars. Contains poem by Frank Ziegler for Flt Lt Jean Offenberg, both of 609 Sqn in Battle of Britain, and "High Flight" by John Magee. Good list of reference acknowledgments and dates of original appearances.
Eades, P/O G. *Thy Muse Hath Wings.* Oxford: Pen in Hand Publishing.
E.B.B., ed. *Winged Words: Our Airmen Speak for Themselves.* London: Heinemann, 1941.

Fassam, Flt Lt Thomas. *The Shrapnel in the Tree*. London: Hand and Flower Press, 1945. Poems from 1940–41.

Fitz Roy, Olivia. *Selected Poems*. Privately printed. Author was in WRNS as fighter direction officer at Yeovilton.

Lucas, Laddie. ed. *Out of the Blue*. London: Hutchinson, 1985. Contains many verses.

Magee, John Gillespie. "High Flight." In *More Poems from the Forces*. London, 1943. The poet was in training in 1940; he was killed on active service at RAF Digby 1941 and is buried there. RCAF. This is the poem quoted by Ronald Reagan after the Challenger space disaster.

Marsden, Eric. *Songs of a Sad Sack: The Songs We Sang*. Chichester: Tangmere Museum of Military Aviation, 1987. RAF personnel, WW2.

Richardson, Anthony. *Because of These*. London: Hodder and Stoughton, 1964.

Sutton, Gp Capt Barry. *The Summer of the Firebrand*. Poetry for the Battle of Britain. A badly burned pilot who wrote of the summer of 1940.

Ward-Jackson, C. H., ed. *Airman's Song Book*. London: Sylvan Press, 1945. The music editor was C. H. Leighton-Lucas, who wrote many wartime musicals and songs. Ward-Jackson also wrote *It's a Piece of Cake*: or RAF Slang Made Easy and several short story collections.

Weir, A.N.C., F/O DFC. *Verses of a Fighter Pilot*. London: Faber and Faber, 1941.

If copies of station magasines can be located, there are several poems of different kinds and dates contained in the editorial. An example would be *Wing* magasine, copies of which are at the RAF Museum, Hendon. But unless others of this type have been lodged at the British Library's Newspaper Section, which is unlikely, they can only be found by chance in the station's operational record books, in AIR 28 at the PRO. Another source is The Poetry Library, Level 5, Red Side, Royal Festival Hall, London SE1 8XX, which collects twentieth century poetry in Britain. Membership is free, and the library is open seven days a week, 11:00 A.M. to 8:00 P.M.

POLAND

Fiedler, Arkady. *Squadron 303*. London: Peter Davies, 1942. Story of a Polish fighter squadron with the RAF.

Ingham, M. J. *The Polish Air Force in Lincolnshire 1940-47*.

Jan: Portrait of a Polish Airman by His English Wife. London: Geoffrey Bless, 1944.

Jaworzyn, J. F. *PAF—No Place to Land*. London: William Kimber, 1984. 311 Squadron Coastal Command.

Marsh, L. G. *Polish Wings over Britain*. Max Love Publishing, 1943.

Polish Air Force Association. *Destiny Can Wait*. London: Heinemann, 1949. First of the Allied Air Forces to go into combat; 1939 to 1940, Battle of Britain.

Polish Community. *Passport to Exile*. London: Hammersmith and Fulham, 1988. Community History Series. A dual language publication. Most of these titles are in English but a bibliography in Polish may be obtained from the Polish Air Force Association, Collingham Gardens, Kensington, London; the Polish Institute, King Street Hammersmith, London; or the Hammersmith and Fulham Public Libraries.

RADAR

Clayton, Aileen. *The Enemy Is Listening*. London: Hutchinson, 1980. Story of the RAF's Y units. Author was the first WAAF to be commissioned as an Intelligence Officer. Comprehensive bibliography, notes, sources with PRO references.

Johnson, Brian. *The Secret War*. London: BBC, 1978. Good chapter on WAAFs in the Battle of Britain and their work in radar. Well illustrated and with good reference notes.

Jones, R. V. *Most Secret War*. London: Hamish Hamilton, 1978.

Kemp, Sqn Ldr'. John. "*Off to War with 054*." Braunton, Devon: Merlin, 1989. Author was a Battle of Britain pilot. This is a good account of his later duties, as part of a radar unit in France.

Lewin, Ronald. *Ultra Goes to War*. London: Hutchinson, 1978. There are, says the author, over 60,000 books and articles on this and related topics. As well as his own bibliography he mentions British and American Official Histories; Ultra Signals in the PRO are in DEF/ E 3, in which there may be more of use and interest.

ROLLS OF HONOUR

These are the roll calls of the names of the dead. They list, usually, those killed in action and those who died on active service. Those who died having left the RAF, after the war or as a later result of the war, are in the In Memoriam records. Many Squadrons and Groups made and kept their own rolls, but there was no official ruling. Details of where these are can often be found at the PRO.

The Roll of the Battle of Britain is in the RAF Chapel in Westminster Abbey, and there is a copy at the RAF Museum at Hendon. A Book of Remembrance is at St Clement Danes RAF Church in the Strand, London.

Some squadrons lodged their own roll in churches associated with them and of particular significance, such as that at St Eval in Cornwall, which commemorates all who served there. There is one for 247 Squadron at High Ercall in Shropshire. But as these cover a wide range of dates, they do not solely represent the Battle. There is further specific information in Winston G. Ramsey, ed., *The Battle of Britain, Then and Now*.

The most comprehensive index is with the Commonwealth War Graves Commission at Maidenhead in Berkshire, from where can be bought its various regional and alphabetical registers, including that of Runnymede for those of no known grave.

There is a Bomber Command roll for the Groups which served in the area in Lincoln Cathedral. A complete list of those who served in the Battle of Britain may be found in the Battle of Britain Pilots Association's lists and in Derek Wood and Derek Dempster's *The Narrow Margin*.

SALES

From time to time the main auction houses as well as other smaller or local firms hold sales of aircraft and flying ephemera. Of these, it is worth getting the catalogues of the following:

Christie's, 85 Old Brompton Road, London SW7 3LD. For example, the sale of 28 April 1990 at Duxford included aircraft from the collection of the late Hon. Patrick Lindsay as well as pictures, books, photographs and a Spitfire replica prototype.

Sotheby's, 34–35 New Bond Street, London W1A 2AA. See medals, etc.

Others include Bonhams, Phillips, and Dowell Lloyd. But do not neglect aeromarts, often held on old airfields, or that annually at Tangmere, and the periodic Ministry of Defence sales.

SLANG

Bowyer, Chaz. *Royal Air Force Handbook 1939–45*. London: Ian Allan, 1984. Has good list of operational code names. List of personnel awarded the VC 1939–45. Good bibliography and biographies. Similar abbreviation lists often explain slang.

Ward-Jackson, C.H., ed. *An Airman's Song Book*. London: Blackwood, 1967.

———. *It's a Piece of Cake, or RAF Slang Made Easy*. London: Sylvan Press.

SOUTH AFRICAN AIR FORCE

There were South Africans in many squadrons, usually described as such. At the PRO South African Squadrons are in AIR 27 and in AIR 54 on microfilm.

SPITFIRES

Although there were more Hurricanes in the Battle, the Spitfire has the most popularity, possibly because of its more graceful lines, or it might even be because the Germans found it easier to call "Achtung! Spitfeur!" across the air waves. The honours on both are equally divided. In this writer's opinion, the best book on each is *Spitfire: The History* by Eric B. Morgan and Edward Shacklady (Stamford, Lincs: Key Publishing, 1987), the ultimate Spitfire reference book and encyclopedia, and *The Hawker Hurricane*, by Francis K. Mason (Bourne End, Bucks: Aston Publications, 1987).

Allward, Maurice, with Ted Hooton. *Air Pictorial* (September 1975). On high claims in Battle 15 September 1940. It is easy to criticise these high claims if one was not flying at 400 mph in highly maneuverable conditions. Easier still when the need to boost morale, civilian and military, is not given the necessary importance.

Andrews, C. F., and E. B. Morgan. *Supermarine Aircraft Since 1914*. London: Putnam, 1987.

Anthony, C. "From Spitfires to Spads." *Air Mail* 5, no. 2 (1953).

Beccles, Gordon. *Birth of a Spitfire*. London: Collins, 1941.

Bowyer, Chaz. *Spitfire*. London: William Kimber.

Bowyer, Michael J. F. *The Spitfire, 50 Years On*. Wellingborough, Northants: Patrick Stephens.

Crook, Flt Lt David M. *Spitfire Pilot*. London: Faber and Faber 1942; London: White Lion, 1976. Story of 609 Sqn at Middle Wallop 1940. Killed 1944; see Winston G. Ramsey, ed., *Battle of Britain, Then and Now*.

Curtiss, Lettice. *A Spitfire Flies Again*. Olney, Bucks: Nelson and Saunders, 1971. Author was an ATA pilot and Spit PRX! was flown in 1948. See also *The Forgotten Pilots*.

Duncan-Smith, Gp Capt W.G.G. *Spitfire into Battle*. London: John Murray, 1981; London: Hamlyn, 1983.

Ellan, Sqn Ldr B. J. (pseud.). *Experiences of a Fighter Pilot*. London: John Murray, 1942.

Flack, Jeremy. *Spitfire, a Living Legend*. London: Osprey.

Henshaw, Alex. *Sigh for a Merlin: Testing the Spitfire*. London: John Murray, 1979.

Hooton, T. *Spitfire Special*. London: Ian Allan, 1972.

Houlton, Johnnie. *Spitfire Strikes, an NZ Fighter Pilot's Story*. London: John Murray, 1985.

Johnstone, Air Vice Marshal Sandy. *Spitfire into Battle*. London: Grafton, 1988. Author was in 602 Sqn at Westhampnett, Sussex.

Lane, B. J. *Spitfire*. London: John Murray, 1942.

Masters, David. *So Few*. London: Eyre and Spottiswoode, 1941, 1946. Corgi, 1956. Miscellaneous real life experiences.

Oxspring, Bobby, Gp Capt DFC/2 bars AFC. *Spitfire Command*. London: William Kimber, 1984.

Price, Alfred. *The Hardest Day: 18 August 1940*. London: Macdonald and Jane's, 1979. Attacks on Biggin Hill and Kenley.

———. *Spitfire at War*. London: Ian Allan, 1974.

———. *The Spitfire Story*. London: Arms and Armour Press, 1986. 300 illustrations.

Quill, Jeffrey, OBE AFC FRAeS. *Spitfire: A Test Pilot's Story*. London: John Murray.

———, with Sebastian Cox. *The Spitfire: Birth of a Legend*. London: Quiller Press, 1986.

Riley, Gordon, and Gordon Trant. *Spitfire Survivors Round the World*. Bourne End: Aston Publications.

Robertson, Bruce. *Spitfire: The Story of a Famous Fighter*. London: Harleyford Publications, 1960; London: Arms and Armour, 1962.

Rolls, Flt Lt W. T., DFC DFM AE. *Spitfire Attack*. London: William Kimber, 1987. Written by a Sgt/pilot, one of the often unsung heroes. In 72 Sqn at Biggin Hill, and at Hornchurch with 122 Squadron. No index but good extracts from his own log.

Slack, Tom. *Happy Is the Day: A Spitfire Pilot's Story*. United Writers Publications Ltd. Title comes from song "happy is the day, when an airman gets his pay." About 41 Squadron, 1940-45; cartoon illustrated.

Smith, Ted, DFC. *Spitfire Diary*. London: William Kimber, 1988.

Spitfire. Special 50th anniversary publication by Portsmouth and Sunderland Newspapers PLC. Portsmouth, September 1990.

Spitfire: The Perfect Lady. Video. 1990.
Vader, John. *Spitfire*. London: Pan Books, 1972.

It is impossible to do justice to the full list of published titles on either aircraft. Refer to subject index at British Library, London. See also AIRCRAFT; BIOGRAPHIES AND PERSONALITIES; COLLECTIONS sections in this volume.

STAMPS

First day covers: See RAF Museum, Hendon, catalogue of flown covers. First published in 1974 and regularly updated, it gives a potted history of stamps, squadrons, people and events, how cover was flown, and so on. Collectors' items.

VIDEOS AND CASSETTES

Producers and Distributors

Aray Films, 63a Ambleside Avenue, Telescombe Cliffs, Newhaven, Sussex BN9 7LN.

AVI, 14 Chepstow Place, Trowbridge, Wilts BA14 9TA. WW2 videos including *Spitfire*.

Aviation Video Library, Dept. F, Kelly House, Warwick Rd., Tunbridge Wells, Kent TN1 1 BR.

Davies, P.O. Box 18, Wallasey, Merseyside, C44 9HD.

D D Distribution, 49 St. Peters Street, London Nl 8JP.

ESP Ltd. (Videos), Archway House, Fairford Rd., Goring on Thames, Berks, RG8 OE4.

Flight Stream, Dept. F1, Tilehurst, Reading, Berks.

International Historic Films Inc., Box 89035, Chicago, Ill. 60629.

RAF Museum Shop, Hendon, with Thorn EMI. *Spitfire* and others. Also has *RAF in Action* (64 Squadron), *History of the RAF*, *Prelude to War*, *Battle of Britain* (U.S. documentary), and many more.

RAF Museum Shop, Hendon, with *After the Battle Magasine*. *Shipbusters*, *Fighter Pilots* (Battle of Britain), *The Eight Days* (Vls), *Ferry Pilot* (ATA pilots).

John Tansley Video, 10 Tanyard, Sandhurst, Cranbrook, Kent.

The Imperial War Museum's own video of the Battle of Britain is on show daily. Other videos are on sale in the shop.

Film and video distributors and addresses where such products can be bought change often, like those of bookshops. Many are stocked in unexpected places and may be bought secondhand. Check addresses in back pages of flying magasines before writing or visiting.

The RAF Careers and Information Service, London, also has films and videos which may be borrowed by special arrangement.

Cassettes and Films

Battle of Britain. Audio cassette by Sir Anthony Quayle. Available from Enigma, P.O. Box 21, Stroud, Glos GL6 Box 21.

Battle of Britain. Film first made in 1969, shown on TV September 1989 for the 50th anniversary of the outbreak of war. See also how the film was made in *Fly Past* for September 1989.

Over the Year: Story of RAF Manston. Audiocassette by Audio Theatre, Sandwich, Kent.

The Glorious Years. Audiocassette by Audio Theatre, Sandwich, Kent.

WAAFs (WOMEN'S AUXILIARY AIR FORCE)

There have not been a great many books written about the WAAFs, and records about them at the Public Record Office are equally difficult to locate, but they played a great part in the Battle of Britain. What there is available is not particularly relevant to the Battle in the air, but they kept aircraft flying and guided them via the various Control Rooms attached to each Sector. Their names and duties must be looked for in the Appendix volumes of the squadrons, units and stations on which they served during that period. Daily Routine and Movement orders, as well as Nominal Rolls, are the main source, which, if found, are in PRO AIR 28 and 29. Documents on the WAAF Directorate are in PRO AIR 24/1640, 1641 and 1642. Most WAAF name records are not in individual book form but are found scattered through the records in general, in the class section AIR at the PRO. The RAF Museum at Hendon has artifacts and pictorial examples.

Babington-Smith, Constance. *Evidence in Camera.* Newton Abbot, Devon: David and Charles, 1957; London: Chatto and Windus, 1974. Discovery, on PRU photos May 1942, of the Peenemunde V rocket ranges.

Beaumont, Kathleen Bentley. *Partners in Blue.* London: Hutchinson, 1943.

———. *Wings on Her Shoulder.* London: Hutchinson, 1943. Reminiscences of a WAAF Flight Officer.

Coltishall—Dover AMES (Air Ministry Experimental Station) Appendix XI, AIR 24/1641–46. This is an interesting record of WAAF units, mainly on radar and similar units, kept and compiled by the women themselves. It includes stations at Done Hill, Berwickshire, Helensburg, Dumbarton, Stoke Holy Cross, Kinloss, Pucklechurch, Boscombe Down, Upavon, Padgate, Marham, Mildenhall, Debden, Farnborough, Honington, Feltwell, Cosford, and Peterborough. It covers 1940–43, and those in the south may have Battle references and background.

WAAF School of Administration. Stoke Orchard. AIR 29/1125.

WAAF Depot. AIR 29/481.

WAAF Historical Record. AIR 16/887, 888, 889, 890.

WAAF Historical Branch narrative. AIR 2/4026 and AIR 6/39.

In PRO, see AIR Class records under such subjects as SSQ (Station Sick Quarters) (in station records AIR 28 and 29); Balloon Command; Radar or AMES records; Control Rooms at HQ or in Air 29 under description; Code and

Cypher Sections; Schools, Officers School at Windermere; Station X at Bletchley Park. There are also WAAF records in AIR 2 Index. ATA records are in AVIA files at the PRO.

"Daughter Come Home." Talk on Channel 4 BBC Radio about WAAF and ATA, 25 May 1989.

Escott, Sqn Ldr Beryl E. *Women in Air Force Blue.* Wellingborough: Patrick Stephens, 1989.

Johnson, Brian. *The Secret War.* London: BBC, 1978. Chapter on WAAF plotters in radar.

Kidd, Janet Aitken. *The Beaverbrook Girl: Growing Up in the 20s.* London: Collins, 1987. Her father was Minister of Aircraft Production, her brother the fighter pilot Max Aitken. She learnt to fly a helicopter and married a pilot.

Pushman, Muriel Gane. *We All Wore Blue.* London: Robson Books, 1989.

Settle, Mary Lee. *All the Brave Promises.* London: Pandora, 1984. About WAAF ACW2 2146391.

Terry, Roy. *Women in Khaki.* London: Columbus Book, 1988. The story of the British woman soldier. Has sections on the WAAF and WRAF. Well illustrated, with good bibliography and index.

Balloon Command (AIR 13 and AIR 24) controlled the barrage balloons, which were anchored at a given height over towns and cities, airfields and ships, so that intruding fighters could not fly in low enough to attack. Though raised and lowered according to need, the defence was not always successful. These units, as were some AA guns, were often manned by women. Disbanded 1995.

WOMEN

Babington-Smith, Constance. *Amy Johnson, Aviation Pioneer.* Cambridge: Patrick Stephens, 1985. Author discovered the Peenemunde flying bomb sites on photographs. Amy Johnson, civilian air ace, was with ATA during the war.

Curtis, Lettice. *The Forgotten Pilots.* Olney: Nelson and Saunders, 1971. No bibliography, but good cross referencing of statistics and names. Story of the pilots of the ATA (Air Transport Auxiliary).

Ewing, Elizabeth. *Women in Uniform.* London: Batsford, 1987. Costume through the ages.

Hall, "Archie." *We Also Were There.* WAAFs in Bomber Command.

King, Alison. *Golden Wings.* London: C. Arthur Pearson, 1956. Women ferry pilots of the ATA.

Lomax, Judy. *Hanna Reitsch: Flying for the Fatherland.* London: John Murray. Germany's flying heroine of the Luftwaffe. Good German bibliography.

———. *Women of the Air.* London: John Murray, 1986. Good bibliography.

Lovell, Mary S. *Straight on Till Morning.* Biography of Beryl Markham, flyer of the 1930s.

Marchant, Hilda. *Women and Children Last.* London: Victor Gollancz, 1941. A woman reporter's account of the Battle of Britain.

Markham, Beryl. *West with the Night.* 1920–30s aviatrix.

Moggridge, Jackie. *Woman Pilot.* London: Michael Joseph, 1957.
Pushman, Muriel Gane. *We All Wore Blue.* London: Robson Books, 1989.
Stobbs, Anne. Dear *One-oh-Eight.* Tring, Herts: Hertfords Literary Services, 1990. WAAFs on a radar station.
Taller, Jane, with Michael Vaughan-Rees. *Women in Uniform.* London: Macmillan. Fashions in forces' uniforms.
Taylor, Eric. *Women Who Went to War, 1938–46.* London: Grafton, 1989. Good bibliography. Foreword by Air Commodore Dame Felicity Hill, DBE WRAF. Taylor was an RAF Sqn Ldr.
Tilbury, Ann. *The Battle of Britain.* London and New York: Simon and Schuster, 1990. Reprint of a 1981 children's book, with illustrations by Michael Turner, President of the Guild of Aviation Artists.
Waller, Jane. *Women in Uniform.* London: Macmillan, 1989.

Women also replaced men in aircraft production factories. Though they may not be listed by name, background detail may be found in Ministry of Aircraft Production (MAP) files at the PRO. Women took over from men on the land as well as in the Services and munitions factories. Land Army details and records are in Ministry of Agriculture and Fisheries (Food)—MAF class files (PRO). Many a Battle of Britain pilot was saved from his plane or parachute drop by Land Army girls. Land Army records can be found in MAF 59 and 65–81 at the PRO. Farm Survey Maps are in MAF32 and 73.

5

Alphabetical Listing by Author

Since the rest of the book is more or less self-explanatory by subject, most of the books contained therein are in this alphabetical list, but some are not included for sheer lack of space. Not included also are books of general guidance, such as *Burke's Peerage* and *Debrett's Peerage and Baronetage*, titles by HMSO, and newspapers. Nor are films and music. All these are in their classified sections, as is material at the Public Record Office. Should readers require further guidance, an sase will bring more information and advice on specialised RAF research.

The Imperial War Museum, located on Lambeth Road, London SE1 6HZ, was the old Bethlehem Hospital or Asylum for disturbed patients. It is now a museum and library containing artifacts and history of two world wars. It offers an important research facility for the serious researcher, and most titles listed here can be located in the Department of Printed Books. There are useful Departments of Film, Sound, Art, Photographs and much more from 1914 to the present day. Notice must be given 24 hours in advance and appointments made, as seating is limited. Entrance is free but there is a charge for the Museum. The Museum is closed the last two weeks of November, but there is a limited service available on Saturdays.

The Commonwealth War Graves Commission Indexes by cemetery are held here. The Museum's outstation of what was RAF Duxford contains aircraft of all kinds and their support equipment. RAF Duxford was closed as an operational airfield in 1961.

Abbott, P. E., and J. M. A. Tamplin. *British Gallantry Awards*. London: Guinness Superlatives, 1971. Describes and illustrates decorations.

Adams, Perry. *Hurricane Squadron: Story of 87 Squadron, 1939–41*. New Malden, Surrey: Air Research Publications, 1988.

Addington, Gurth. Odd Bods at War, 1939–45. Kinkumber, New South Wales 1990.

Air Ministry. *The Battle of Britain*. Department for Air Training, Pamphlet 156. London: MoD, 1943.

Allen, Wg Cdr Hubert Raymond "Dizzy." *The Battle for Britain*. London: Arthur Barker, 1973.

———. *Who Won the Battle of Britain?* London: Panther, 1976.

Allward, Maurice. *Hurricane Special*. London: Ian Allan, 1975.

Andrews, C. F., and E. B. Morgan. *Supermarine Aircraft Since 1914*. London: Putnam, 1987.

Ansel, Walter. *Hitler Confronts England*. Durham, NC: Duke University Press, 1960.

Anthony, C. "From Spitfires to Spads." *Air Mail* 5, no 2 (1953).

Anthony, Gordon, and MacAdam, John. *Air Aces*. London: Home and Van Thal, 1944.

———. "Air Defences of the Port of London." *PL Association Monthly* (May 1945).

———. *The Battle of Britain, a short history*. London: Air Ministry Public Relations, 1960.

Anthony, Harold. *Camera above the Clouds*. 2 vols. Shrewsbury: Air Life Publications. Photos by Charles E. Brown.

Ardizzione, Edward. *Diary of a War Artist*. London: Bodley Head, 1974.

Armitage, Sqn Ldr Dennis. "The Battle of Britain." *The Elevator* (journal of the Lancashire Aero Club) (Spring/Autumn 1958).

Asher, Lee. *Blitz on Britain*.

Ashman, R. V. *Spitfire Against the Odds*. Author enlisted at age 16 in 1938.

Ashworth, Chris. *Encyclopedia of Modern Royal Air Force Squadrons*. Wellingborough, Northants: Patrick Stephens, 1989. Although about existing RAF squadrons, their 1940 history is included.

———. *The Military Airfields of the South West*. Vol. 5: *Action Stations*. Wellingborough: Patrick Stephens and Thorsons, 1982.

———. *The Military Airfields of the South and South East*. Vol. 9: *Action Stations*. Wellingborough: Patrick Stephens and Thorsons, 1985.

Atkins, Peter. *Buffoon in Flight*. Johannesburg: Ernest Stanton, 1979. 24 Sqn.

Austin, A. B. *Fighter Command*. London: Victor Gollancz, 1941.

Babington-Smith, Constance. *Amy Johnson*. London: Patrick Stephens, 1985.

———. *Evidence in Camera*. London: Chatto and Windus, 1974.

Bader, Douglas. *Fight for the Sky*. London: Sidgwick and Jackson, 1975.

Bagley, J. A. *A Gazeteer of Hampshire Aerodromes*. Hampshire Field Club and Archaeological Society, 1972.

Bailey, Jim. *The Sky Suspended*. London: Hodder and Stoughton, 1965.

Baker, E. C. R. *Fighter Aces of the RAF, 1939–45*. London: William Kimber, 1962.

Balfour of Inchrye, Lord. *Biggin Hill and Other Poems*.

Baldwin, Hanson W. *The Crucial Years*. London: Weidenfeld and Nicholson, 1976. From parts originally in the *New York Times*. *Balfour Papers*. House of Lords Record Office.

Barbas, Bernd. *Planes of the Luftwaffe Fighter Aces*. Germany.

Barclay, Glen St. J. *Their Finest Hour*. London: Weidenfeld and Nicholson, 1977.

Barclay, R. A. George, OFC. *Fighter Pilot*. London: William Kimber, 1976. Self portrait edited by Dr. Humphrey Wynn, Air Historical Branch historian. See also Wynn's article in *RAF Quarterly* (September 1974), commemorating the Battle of Britain.

Barker, A. J. *Dunkirk, the Great Escape.* London: Dent, 1977.

Barker, Felix. "Twenty Four Hours That Saved Britain." *London Evening News*, September 12–17, 1940.

Barker, Ralph. *Aviator Extraordinary: The Sidney Cotton Story.* 1969.

———. *Children of the Benares.* London: Methuen, 1987.

———. *Down in the Drink.* London: Chatto and Windus, 1955.

———. "Scramble to Glory." *Sunday Express*, 9 September 1980.

———. *That Eternal Summer: Unknown Stories from the Battle of Britain.* London: Collins, 1990.

Barnes, D. G. *Cloud Cover.* London: Rich and Cowan, 1943. Recollections of an Intelligence Officer.

Barrymaine, Norman. *The Story of Peter Townsend.* London: Peter Davies, 1958.

Barthropp, Wg Cdr Patrick. *Paddy: The Life and Times of Wg Cdr Paddy Barthropp.* London: Baker, 1987. See also *Sunday Telegraph*, September 1988.

Bartley, Anthony. *Smoke Trails in the Sky: 92 Squadron.* London: William Kimber, 1956, 1986.

Bartz, Karl. *Swastika in the Sky.* London: William Kimber, 1956.

Batchelor, Jack, with Chris Chant. *Fighter.* Newton Abbot Devon: David and Charles, 1988.

Bateman, Dennis C. *Home Commands of RAF since 1918.* London: MoD/AHB, 1978.

Bates, H. E. *War Pictures by British Artists.* Oxford: Oxford University Press, 1942.

"The Battle of Britain." Icare, *Revues des Pilotes de Ligne*, no. 35–36 (Autumn/Winter 1965). English and French text.

———. *The Battle of Britain 40th Anniversary Reunion: The Bump-RAF, Biggin Hill.* London: Nicholas Wright, September 1980.

Baumbach, Werner. *Broken Swastika.* London: Robert Hale, 1960, 1974.

———. "Why We Lost." *Royal Air Force Review* 7, no. 12 (1952–53).

Baur, Lt Gen Hans. *Hitler's Pilot.* London: Frederic Muller, 1950, 1958. See also AIR 16/619 at PRO.

BBC (TV film). *Missing.* BBC's Written Archives Centre, wartime radio broadcasts. Story of Hugh Beresford, killed 7 September 1940.

Beamish, Gp Capt Victor, DSO DFC AFC. *Wings Aflame.* London: William Kimber, 1986.

Beamont, Wg Cdr Roland. *Fighter Test Pilot.* Wellingborough: Patrick Stephens, 1987.

———. *My Part of the Sky.* Wellingborough: Patrick Stephens, 1989.

———. *Phoenix into Ashes.* London: William Kimber, 1968.

Beaty, D., and M. Beaty. *Wings of the Morning.* London: Macmillan, 1982. Fiction.

Beauman, Kathleen Bentley. *Partners in Blue.* London: Hutchinson, 1943.

———. *Wings on Her Shoulder.* London: Hutchinson, 1943.

Beaverbrook Papers. House of Lords Record Office, London. Lord Beaverbrook was Minister for Aircraft Production.

Beckles, Gordon. *Birth of a Spitfire.* London: Collins, 1941.

Beedle, James. *43 Squadron.* Beamont Aviation, 1966. Story of The Fighting Cocks, 1916–1966, RFC/RAF.

Bekker, Cajus. *The Luftwaffe War Diaries.* London: Macdonald, 1965–67.

Benes, Bohus. *Wings in Exile.* London: Czech Independent Weekly, 1942.

Bennett, AVM D. C. T. *Pathfinder.* London: Frederick Muller, 1958; London: Goodall, 1959. See also Alan Bramson's *Master Airman* (Shrewsbury: Airlife, 1985).
Bevis, Lewis S., ed. *Odd Bods at War, 1939–45: Aussies in the RAF.* Kinkumber, NSW, 1990. Australians in the RAF.
Bickers, R. T. *Ginger Lacey, Fighter Pilot.* London: Robert Hale, 1962.
Birkby, Carel. *Dancing in the Skies.* Capetown: Howard Timmins, 1982.
Bishop, Edward. *The Battle of Britain.* London: Allen and Unwin, 1960.
———. *The Guinea Pig Club.* London: Macmillan, 1963. How Archibald MacIndoe saved burned pilots. Invaluable.
———. *Hurricane.* Shrewsbury: Airlife, 1986.
Blake (pseudo. for Wg Cdr Ronald Adams). *Readiness at Dawn.* London: Brown Watson. Fiction.
———. *We Rendezvous at Ten.* London: Gollancz, 1942.
Bloemertz, G. *Heaven Next Stop.* 1953.
Blond, Georges. *Born to Fly.* London: Souvenir Press, 1956.
Bolitho, Hector. *Combat Report.* London: Batsford, 1943.
———. *Penguin in the Eyrie.* London: Hutchinson, 1955.
Boorman, H. R. P. *Hell's Corner, 1940.* Maidstone: Kent Messenger, 1942.
Boorman, H. R. P., and H. R. Long. *Recalling the Battle of Britain.* Maidstone: Kent Messenger, 1965. This newspaper was in the front line.
Bowen, Elizabeth. *Heat of the Day.* Jonathan Cape, 1949. A novel of the 1940s.
Bowman, Gerald. *Jump For It: The Caterpillar Club.* London: Evans, 1955.
Bowman, Martin W. *Classic Fighter Aircraft.* London: William Kimber, 1976.
———. *Bomber Group at War.* London: Ian Allan, 1981
Bowyer, Chaz. *The Age of the Biplane.* London: William Kimber.
———. *Air War over Europe, 1939–45.* London: William Kimber, 1981.
———. *The Beaufighter.* London: Ian Allan, 1976. Heavily armed fighter, 1940–50.
———. *Beaufighter at War.* London: William Kimber, 1976.
———. *Bomber Group at War.* London: Ian Allan, 1981.
———. *Coastal Command at War.* London: Ian Allan, 1979.
———. *Eugene Esmond, VC, DSO, FAA.* London: William Kimber, 1972.
———. *Fighter Command 1936–68.* London: J. M. Dent, 1980.
———. *Fighter Pilots of the RAF 1939–45.* London: William Kimber, 1980.
———. *For Valour: The Air VCs.* London: William Kimber, 1978. Reprinted 1986.
———, ed. *Hurricane at War.* London: Ian Allan, 1975.
———. *Images of Air War, 1935–45.* London: Batsford, 1983.
Bowyer, Michael J. F. *Aircraft for the Few.* Wellingborough: Patrick Stephens, 1991.
———. *The Battle of Britain: 50 Years On.* Cambridge: Patrick Stephens, 1990.
———. *Duxford: Its First Year of War.* East Anglian Aviation Society, 1974.
———. *The Military Airfields of East Anglia.* Vol. 1. Action Stations. Wellingborough: Patrick Stephens and Thorsons, 1979.
———. *The Military Airfields of the Central Midlands.* Vol. 6. Action Stations. Wellingborough: Patrick Stephens and Thorsons, 1983.
———. *RAF Camouflage of World War II.* Cambridge: Air Fix Products Ltd., Stephens, 1976.
———. *The Spitfire, 50 Years On.* Wellingborough: Patrick Stephens, 1985.
Boyle, Andrew. *Trenchard.* London: Collins, 1962.
Braham, Wg Cdr J. R. D. *Scramble.* London: William Kimber, 1961, 1987.

Bramson, Alan. *Master Airman.* Shrewsbury: Airlife, 1985. About AVM D. C. T. Bennett.

Brandon, L. *Night Flyer.* London: William Kimber, 1961. Nightfighting was only in its experimental training infancy during the year of the Battle. This explains why and how it developed.

Braybrook, K. *Wingspan: A History of RAF Debden,* RAF Debden, 1956.

Brickhill, Paul. *Escape or Die.* London: Evans, 1952.

———. *Escape to Danger.* London: Faber, 1946.

———. *The Great Escape.* London: Collins.

———. *Reach for the Sky.* London: Collins, 1954.

Brittain, Vera. *England's Hour.* London: Macmillan, 1941.

Brookes, Andrew J. *Fighter Squadron at War.* London: Ian Allan, 1980.

———. *Photo Reconnaissance Unit.* London: Ian Allan, 1975.

Brooks, R. J. *From Moths to Merlins.* Story of West Malling airfield.

Brown, Anthony Cave. *Bodyguard of Lies.* London: Comet, W. H. Allen, 1986.

Brown, Vincent. *The Way Back.* London: Cassel, 1957.

Bruce, John M. Foreword to *British Aviation Colours of World War II.* London: Arms and Armour Press.

Bryant, Sir Arthur. *The Turn of the Tide, 1939–45.* London: Collins, 1957. One of a series.

Burn, Michael. *Mary and Richard.* London: Andre Deutsch, 1988.

———. *Spitfire! Spitfire!* Poole: Blandford Press.

Burt, Kendal, and James Leasor. *The One That Got Away.* London: Collins, 1956.

Butler, P. H., ed. *British Isles, Airfield Guide.* Merseyside Aviation Society, 1976.

Callaway, Tim. *Battle of Britain Project Book.* London: Headway, Hodder and Stoughton, 1989.

Cameron, Dugald. *Glasgow's Own: 602 Squadron, 1925–57.* Glasgow: Squadron Prints, 1988.

Cannadine, David. *Blood, Toil, Tears and Sweat: Winston Churchill's Famous Speeches.* London: Cassell PLC, 1989.

Capka, Joe. *Red Sky at Night.* London: Blond, 1958.

Carne, Daphne. *The Eyes of the Few.* London: Macmillan, 1960.

Chambers, Aidan, comp. *Fighters in the Sky.* London: Macmillan, 1976. For young people.

Channon, Sir Henry. *Chips.* Ed. Robert Rhodes James. London: Penguin, 1970. Diary of Sir Henry "Chips" Channon, 1940.

Cheshire, Gp Capt Leonard. *Bomber Pilot.* London: Hutchinson, 1943.

"Chiefy" B. (pseud.) *"Goings On."* RAF Gravesend, 1973.

Childers, J. S. *War Eagles.* London: Heinemann, 1943.

Chinnery, Phil. *Gate Guards.* Manchester: World Books.

Chisholm, R. *Cover of Darkness.* London: Chatto and Windus, 1953.

Churchill, Winston. *Their Finest Hour.* Boston: Houghton Mifflin, 1949. Churchill was Prime Minister during these crucial years of war. Other books by and about him have important background.

Clark, Ronald W. *The Battle for Britain.* London: George Harrap, 1975. Sixteen weeks that changed the course of history.

Clayton, Aileen. *The Enemy Is Listening.* London: Hutchinson, 1980, 1986.

Clostermann, Pierre. *The Big Show.* London: Chatto and Windus, 1951.

———. *Flames in the Sky*. London: Chatto and Windus, 1952.

Clouston, Air Commodore A. E. *The Dangerous Skies: A Test Pilot's Adventures in Peace and War.* London: Cussell, 1954; Pan, 1956.

Clout, Charles. *Swastika over Sussex.* Tonbridge: Air Britain, 1956.

Cluet, Douglas. *The First, the Fastest and the Famous.* London: Sutton Libraries, 1986. About Croydon Airport.

Cluet D., J. Bogle, and B. Learmonth. *Croydon Airport and the Battle of Britain.* London: Sutton Libraries and Arts Services, 1985.

Cockerell, Geoffrey. *Remembering the Few.* 40th Anniversary, 1980.

Collier, Basil. *The Battle of Britain.* London: Batsford, 1962.

———. *The City that Wouldn't Die.* New York: E. P. Dutton, 1960.

———. *The Defence of the United Kingdom.* London: HMSO, 1957.

———. *Hidden Weapons.* London: Hamilton, 1982.

———. *The Leader of the Few.* London: Jarrolds, 1957.

———, ed. *The Battle of Britain.* London: Jackdaw Publications, Cape, 1969. A collection of contemporary documents.

Collier, Richard. *Eagle Day.* London: Hodder and Stoughton, 1966; J. M. Dent, 1980.

———. *1940: The Work in Flames.* London: Hamilton, 1979; Penguin, 1980.

Collishaw, Air Vice Marshal Raymond, with R. V. Dodds. *Air Command: A Fighter's Story.* London: William Kimber, 1973.

Collyer, David G. *Battle of Britain, Diary of Events.* Maidstone: East Kent Defence Research Group, Kent Aviation Historical Society, 1980.

Colville, Sir John. *The Fringes of Power: Downing Street Diaries.* 2 vols. London: Hodder and Stoughton, 1985. Two volumes giving good background to the period; vol. 1 covers 1939-October 1941. Author was a fighter pilot.

Cooksley, Peter G. *Croydon Airport.* London: Robert Hale, 1983.

———. *1940: The Story of 11 Group, Fighter Command.*

Cooksley, Peter, and Richard Ward. *The Battle of Britain—Hurricane, Spitfire, Messerschmitt Bf 109.* London: Osprey, 1968.

Cooper, Alan W. *Free to Fight Again.* London: William Kimber, 1988. RAF escapes and evasions, 1940–45.

Cooper, Bryan. *Fighter.* London: Macdonald, 1974.

Cooper, Matthew. *The German Air Force, 1933–45.* London: Jane's, 1981.

Copeman, Geoff. *Silksheen.* 1989. 57 and 630 Squadrons.

Coppock, J. T., and Hugh C. Price, eds. *Greater London.* London: Faber, 1964. The title refers to the administrative area outside the central city zone.

Corbell, Peter. "RAF Hornchurch." *Air Britain Digest* 3, nos. 9–10.

Cosgrave, Patrick. *Churchill at War: Alone, 1939–40.* Vol 1. London: Collins, 1974.

Crawley, Aiden. *Escapes from Germany.* London: Collins, 1956.

Crook, Flt Lt D. M. *Spitfire Pilot.* London: Faber and Faber, 1942; London: White Lion, 1976.

Cross and Cockade. *British Airfields on the Continent* 10, no. 4 (1979). This association is at Cragg Cottage, The Craggs, Bramham, Wetherby, W Yorks. Mainly concerned with WWI, it can help with biographies of this generation involved in the Battle of Britain.

Curtis, Lettice. *The Forgotten Pilots.* Olney: Nelson and Saunders, 1971.

———. *A Spitfire Flies Again.* Olney: Nelson and Saunders, 1971.

Czernin, Count Manfred, with Norman L. R. Franks. *Double Mission.* London: William Kimber, 1976. RAF fighter Ace and SOE agent.

Dahl, Roald. *Biography.* London: Jonathan Cape, 1984. Author was a Battle of Britain fighter pilot, now an internationally known writer of short stories.

Darlington, Roger. *Night Hawk.* London: William Kimber, 1985.

Davies, Brian C. *Luftwaffe Aircrews 1940.* London: Arms and Armour Press, 1974.

Deere, Alan C. *Nine Lives.* London: Hodder and Stoughton, 1959.

Deighton, Len. *The Battle of Britain.* London: Jonathan Cape, 1980.

———. *Fighter: The True Story of the Battle of Britain.* London: Panther, 1977.

Divine, David. *The Broken Wing.* London: Hutchinson, 1966.

———. *The Nine Days of Dunkirk.* London: David Higham Associates and White Lion, 1976.

Dixon, J. L. *In All Things First: A History of No 1 Squadron.* Orpington, Kent: Orpington Press, 1954.

Dixon, Ronald, ed. *Echoes in the Sky.* Poole, Dorset: Blandford Press, 1982. Anthology of aviation verse from two world wars. Contains poem by Frank Ziegler for Flt Lt Jean Offenberg, and "High Flight" by John Magee.

Donahue, Art. *Tally Ho!* London: Macmillan, 1943.

Dorling, H. Tapprell. *Ribbons and Medals.* London: Phillips, 1974.

Dorman, Geoffrey. *British Test Pilot.* London: Forbes Robertson, 1950.

Douglas, Sholto. *The Years of Combat.* London: Collins, 1966.

Dowding, Air Chief Marshal Sir Hugh C. T. "The Battle of Britain." Supplement to the *London Gazette*, 11 September 1946. See also PRO AIR 8/863, The Dowding Despatches.

Dowling, C., and N. Frankland, eds. "The Battle of Britain," in *Decisive Battles of the Twentieth Century.* London: Sidgwick and Jackson, 1976.

Downes, Mollie Panter. "London War Notes." *Atlantic Monthly* (1940).

Drew, G. A. *Canada's Fighting Airmen.* Ottawa: Maclean, 1931.

Dudgeon, Air Vice Marshal Tony, CBE DFC. *Luck of the Devil, 1934–41.* Shrewsbury: Airlife, 1985.

———. *Wings Over North Africa.* Shrewsbury: Airlife, 1987. Mainly about middle east but good background to early training.

Dundas, Sir Hugh. *Flying Start: A Fighter Pilot's War Years.* London: Stanley Paul, 1988.

Duncan-Smith, Gp Capt W. G. G. *Spitfire into Battle.* London: John Murray, 1981.

Eades, Robert, and Herbie Knott. *How They Made the Film "Piece of Cake."* London: Boxtree, 1988.

Eagle, P/O G. *Thy Muse Hath Wings.* Oxford: Pen in Hand Publishing, 1951.

Edwards, Gron. *Norwegian Patrol.* Shrewsbury: Airlife, 1985. Graphic and racy story of 233 General Reconnaissance Squadron.

Ellan, Sqn Ldr B. J. *Experiences of a Fighter Pilot.* London: John Murray, 1942.

Ellis, John. *Social History of the Machine Gun.* London: Croom Helm.

Embry. Air Chief Marshal Sir Basil, GCB KBE DSO DFC AFDC. *Mission Completed.* London: Methuen, 1954.

Emory, John. *Source Book of World War II Aircraft.* Poole, Dorset: Blandford Press.

Escott, Sqn Ldr Beryl E. *RAF High Wycombe.* Constitutional Press, 1974.

———. *Women in Air Force Blue.* London: Patrick Stephens, 1989.

Evans, A. J. *The Escapers' Club.* London: Bodley Head. Stories by or about the Club members.

Ewing, Elizabeth. *Women in Uniform.* London: Batsford, 1987.

Fairclough, N. W. *New Zealanders in the Battle of Britain.* Wellington, N. Z.: Department of Internal Affairs, 1950.

Fairfax, E. *Fighter Aircraft.* London: Cassell PLC, 1989.

Fairhall, Lawrence. *British Air Aces.* London: Rolls House, 1944.

Fassam, Flt Lt Thomas. *The Shrapnell in the Tree.* London: Hand and Flower Press, 1945.

Feist, Uwe. *The Fighting ME109.* London: Arms and Armour Press, 1989.

Fellowes, P. F. M. *Britain's Wonderful Air Force, 1943.* London: Odhams, 1942.

Fiedler, Arkady. *Squadron 303.* London: Peter Davies, 1942.

Finn, Sid. *Black Swan: 103 Squadron.* Edenbridge: Newton, 1989. A bomber squadron, 58 years of the RFC and RAF.

Finnie, G. K. "Lessons of the Battle of Britain." *Roundel* 1, no. 6.

Fitzgerald, Percy. *Victoria's London.* London: Alderman Press, 1984.

Fitz Roy, Olivia. *Selected Poems.* Privately printed. Joined WRNS as a fighter direction officer at Yeovilton.

Flack, Jeremy. *Spitfire, a Living Legend.* London: Osprey, 1990.

Fleming, Peter. *Invasion 1940* (British title of *Operation Sea Lion).* London: Hart Davies, 1956; London: White Lion, 1975; London: Pan Books, 1984. Account of the German preparation and British countermeasures. See also biography of Fleming by Rupert Hart-Davies and the difficulties of obtaining documents.

———. *Operation Sea Lion.* New York: Simon and Schuster, 1957.

Foot, M. R. D. SOE: *The Special Operations Executive, 1940-45.* London: BBC, 1984.

Foreman, John. *The Battle of Britain: The Forgotten Months, November–December 1940.* New Malden: Air Research, 1988.

Forrester, Larry. *Fly For Your Life.* London: Muller, 1956. Story of Wg Cdr Bob Stanford Tuck, DSO DFC.

Forsyth, Frederick. *The Shepherd.* London: Hutchinson, 1975. Fiction.

Foster, Reginald. *Dover Front.* London: Secker and Warburg, 1941.

Fox, Edward. *The Battle of Britain.* London: Lutterworth Press, 1969.

Foxley-Norris, Sir Christopher. *Royal Air Force at War.* London: Ian Allan, 1983. Photo research captioned by Chaz Bowyer for the RAF Benevolent Fund.

Fozard, Dr. John W. *Sydney Camm and the Hurricane.* Shrewsbury: Airlife. Master fighter designer and his finest achievement.

Frankland, N., with E. Dowling, eds. "The Battle of Britain." In *Decisive Battles of the Twentieth Century.* London: Sidgwick and Jackson, 1976.

Franks, Norman. *The Battle of Britain.* London: Bison Books, 1981.

———. *Hurricane at War 2.* London: Ian Allan, 1986.

———. *Sky Tiger.* London: William Kimber, 1980. About Sailor Malan.

———. *Valiant Wings.* London: William Kimber, 1988. Battle and Blenheim Squadrons over France, 1940.

Franks, N. L. R. *Aircraft v Aircraft.* New York: Bantam, 1986. Illustrated story of Fighter combat.

———. *A Few of the Few: Battle of Britain.* London: Tandem, 1969. Accounts by Richard Hillary, Hillary St George Saunders, Cajus Bekker. Includes "The Last Enemy" and "The Luftwaffe Diaries." First published by MoI, London, 1941.

———. *Fighter Leader*. London: William Kimber, 1978.
———. *Scramble to Victory: Five Fighter Pilots*. London: William Kimber, 1987.
Fraser, David. *Blitz*. London: Macmillan, 1979.
Fraser, Flt Lt W. *RAF Manston*. RAF Manston, 1969.
Fraser, F/O W. *Manston, the Story of the RAF Station*. Littlebury and Co., 1973.
Freeman, Roger A. *The British Airman*. London: Cassell PLC, 1989. In Experiences of War series, which includes James Lucas, *The British Soldier*, and Kenneth Poolman, *The British Sailor*.
Furniss-Roe, Bill. *Believed Safe*. London: William Kimber, 1987. A fighter pilot's double escape.
Fyson, Nance Lui. *The 1940s*. London: Batsford, 1988.
Galland, Adolf. *The First and the Last*. London: Methuen, 1955.
Gallico, Paul. *The Hurricane Story*. London: Michael Joseph, 1959.
Gardner, C. *AAF*. London: Hutchinson, 1940.
Gee, J. W. *Wingspan*. London.
Gelb, Norman. *Scramble!* London: Michael Joseph, 1986.
Gibbs, AVM Gerald. "The Battle of Britain." *Journal of the United Services Institute of India* 83, pp. 352–53.
———. *Survivor's Story*. London: Hutchinson, 1956.
Gibson, Jeremy, and Colin Rogers. *Coroners' Records in England and Wales*. London: Society of Genealogists, 1987.
Giddings, M. L. *The Return of the Dambusters*. 617 Sqn. Not about the Battle of Britain, but has useful information on the formation of reunions and associations of such aircrew, how and where to find them, and so on.
Gilbert, Martin. *Finest Hour: Winston Churchill, 1939-42*. London: Heinemann, 1983.
Gleave, T. P. *I Had a Row with a German*. London: Macmillan, 1941.
Gleed, Wg Cdr Ian, DFC. *Arise to Conquer*. London: Gollancz, 1942. Dedicated to the ground staff.
Goddard, Sir Victor. *The Skies to Dunkirk: A Personal Memoir*. London: William Kimber, 1982.
Goodson, James. *Tumult in the Clouds*.
Grant, Ian, and Nicholas Madden. *The Countryside at War*. London: Jupiter, 1975.
Graves, Charles. *The Home Guard of Britain*. London: Hutchinson.
Graves, Tim. *Paddy Finucane's Combat Diary*. Liskeard, Cornwall: MvR Publications, 1989. A source book for serious historians. Log Book in PRO AIR 4.
Green, William. *The Augsburg Eagle: Messerschmitt Bf 109*. Bourne End: Aston Publications, 1988. Author is managing editor of *Air International*.
———. *Fighters*. London: Salamander, 1981.
Gribble, Leonard R. *Epics of the Fighting RAF*. London: Harrap, 1943.
Grinsell, Robert. *Messerschmitt Bf 109*. London: Jane's, 1980.
Gunston, Bill. *British Fighters of World War II*. London: Airbooks. See also series article in the magazine *The War in the Air*, 1989.
Hall, "Archie." *We Also Were There*. Braunton: Merlin, 1985.
Hall, Roger. *Clouds of Fear*. Folkestone: Bailey, 1975.
Halley, James. *RAF Units*. Vol. 2, 201–1435 Sqns, 1918-1968. Tonbridge: Air Britain, 1970.
———. *The Squadrons of the Royal Air Force*. Tonbridge: Air Britain, 1980; revised and expanded 1991 as *The Squadrons of the Royal Air Force and Commonwealth*,

1918–1988 (Tonbridge: Air Britain, 1988). Invaluable starting point when squadron number is known; gives date, place and aircraft type.

Halliday, Hugh. *The Canadian Years.* Ottawa: Canadian War Museum, 1987.

Halpenny, Bruce Barrymore. *Action Stations 4: Military Airfields of Yorkshire.* Cambridge: Patrick Stephens, 1982.

———. *Action Stations 2: Military Airfields of Lincolnshire and the East Midlands.* Wellingborough: Patrick Stephens, 1982.

———. *Action Stations 8: Military Airfields of Greater London.* Wellingborough: Patrick Stephens, 1984.

———. *Ghost Stations.* Braunton: Merlin, 1986.

———. *To Shatter the Sky.* Wellingborough: Patrick Stephens. Author's film script, 1984.

Hamilton, James Douglas. *Motive for a Mission.* Edinburgh: Mainstream Publishing, 1974. About Rudolph Hess.

Harley, J. B. *The Historian's Guide to Survey Maps.* London: Standing Conference on Local History for the National Council of Social Services, 1965.

Haslam, Gp Capt E. B. "How Lord Dowding Came to Leave Fighter Command." *Journal of Strategic Studies* (June 1981).

Haughland, Vern. *The Eagle Squadrons: Yanks in the RAF, 1940–42.* Newton Abbot: David and Charles, 1980.

———. *The Eagles' War.* New York: Jason Aronson, 1982.

Hawkins, Leslie C. Brampton. *Eagle Squadron Remembered: Poems, 1938–45.* London: Excalibur Press.

Hayson, G. D. L. "How the Few Saved the Many." *Wings* 9, no. 10 (1950).

Hayward, K., and Norris, P. *A Short History of RAF Northolt.* Chiltern Aviation Society, 1980. Privately published.

Henrey, Madeleine. *Madeleine, Young Wife.* London: J. M. Dent, 1968. War and peace on a farm in Normandy, before and after the war.

Henshaw, Alex. *Sigh for a Merlin: Testing the Spitfire.* London: John Murray, 1979.

Hess, Wolf Rudiger. *My Father, Rudolf Hess.* London: W. H. Allen, 1968. Details of the period leading up to Hess's arrival in the United Kingdom.

Hill, P. *To Know the Sky.* London: William Kimber, 1962.

Hill, Sir Roderick. "The Fighters' Greatest Day." *Journal of the Royal Air Force* 3, no. 5.

Hillier, Caroline. *The Bulwark Shore: Exploring Thanet and the Cinque Ports.* London: Eyre Methuen, 1980; Granada, 1982. Describes in historical detail the ports involved on the southeast coast. Has excellent references to the Battle of Britain, chapter notes and references, good bibliography. The Cinque Ports are Hastings, Sandwich, Dover, Romney, and Hythe. Sir Winston Churchill was Warden of the Cinque Ports.

HMSO. *The Battle of Britain.* London, 1940.

———. *111 Sqn.* London.

———. *151 Sqn.* London.

———. *213 Sqn.* London.

Hoare, John. *Story of the Fleet Air Arm.* London: Michael Joseph, 1976.

———. *Tumult in the Clouds.* London: Michael Joseph.

Hobbs, Anthony. *The Battle of Britain.* Hove, Sussex: Wayland, 1973.

Hodgkinson, Colin. *Best Foot Forward.* London: Odhams Press, 1957. Autobiography of a legless fighter pilot of WWII.

Hodgson, J. R. A. *Letters from a Bomber Pilot.* London: Metheun, 1985.

Holmes, Ray. *Sky Spy.* Shrewsbury: Airlife, 1989. Only partly about the Battle of Britain, but gives good account of air reconnaissance.

Holmes, Richard. *World Atlas of Warfare.* London: Michael Beazley, 1988.

Hooton, T. *Spitfire Special.* London: Ian Allan, 1972.

Hough, Richard. *The Battle of Britain.* New York: Macmillan, 1971. The triumph of the RAF fighter pilots.

———, with Denis Richards. *The Battle of Britain: The Jubilee History.* London: Hodder and Stoughton, 1989.

Houlton, Johnnie. *Spitfire Strikes, an NZ Fighter Pilot's Story.* London: John Murray, 1985. New Zealand pilot.

Howard-Williams, J. *Night Intruder.* Newton Abbot: David and Charles, 1976.

Huart, Capt Victor. "Les Aviateurs Belge à la Bataille d'Angleterre." *VICI,* 17 October 1955. See also his translation of *Lonely Warrior,* by Jean Offenberg, DFC.

Hunt, Leslie. *Defence until Dawn.* Privately printed, 1949.

Hutchinson, Tom. *The Battle of Britain.* London: Purnell, 1960. Illustrated from the film of the same name.

Illingworth, F. *Britain under Shellfire.* London: Hutchinson, 1942.

Imperial War Graves Commission. *Their Names Liveth Forever More.* London: Methuen, 1955. See also the IWGC's Indexes and their Introductions.

Ingham, M. J. *The Polish Air Force in Lincolnshire, 1940-47.* Lincoln: Beckside Design, 1988.

Ishoven, Armand van. *The Luftwaffe in the Battle of Britain.* London: Ian Allan, 1980.

Jackson, R. *A Taste of Freedom.* London: Barker, 1964.

Jackson, Robert. *Fighter Pilots of World War II.* London: Barker, 1976.

Jackson, Ward C. H., ed. *Airman's Song Book.* London: Sylvan Press, 1945. Ward-Jackson was in the RAFVR 1940. This book gives an excellent history of what we sang from WW1 to WW2 and the meanings and reasons behind the words. Has a very good abbreviations list as used in the RAF, index to titles and first lines as well as music. See also the following title.

———. *It's a Piece of Cake: RAF Slang Made Easy.* Sylvan Press. With pen drawings by David Langdon, the cartoonist "Fougasse."

———. *No Bombs at All.* Sylvan Press. Short stories of the Royal Air Force. Wood engravings by Biro.

James, Derek N. *Hawker: An Aircraft Album.* London: Ian Allan, 1972.

Jan: Portrait of a Polish Airman by His English Wife. London: Geoffrey Bless, 1944. Name suppressed for security reasons.

Jefford, Wg Cdr C. G. *Royal Air Force Squadrons.* Shrewsbury: Airlife, 1988. A comprehensive survey of records and equipment of all RAF squadrons and their antecedents since 1912. Comprehensive, detailed and essential for the serious researcher.

Johnson, Brian. *The Secret War.* London: BBC, 1978.

Johnson, F. *RAAF Over Europe.* London: Eyre and Spottiswoode, 1946.

Johnson, "Johnny" E. *One of the Few.* London: William Kimber, 1971.

Johnstone, AVM Sandy. *Enemy in the Sky.* London: William Kimber, 1976.

———. *Spitfire into Battle.* London: Grafton, 1988.

Jones, Wg Cdr Ira. *Tiger Squadron: 74 Squadron.* London: W. H. Allen, 1954.

Jones, R. V. *Most Secret War.* London: Hamish Hamilton, 1978. Invaluable reference work on radar and related subjects. Useful cross references.

Joubert, Air Chief Marshal. "How the Way Was Paved for the Battle of Britain." *RAF Flying Review* 5, no. 2 (1949).

Jubelin, A. *The Flying Sailor.* London: Hurst and Blackett, 1953.

Jullian, Marcel. *The Battle of Britain.* New York: Orion Press, 1965; London: Panther, 1969; London: Cedric Chivers and Jonathan Cape, 1980. The Battle from a Frenchman's point of view.

Kaplan, Philip, and Richard Collier. *The Few: Summer 1940.* London: Cassell PLC, 1989.

Kay, AVM C. E. *The Restless Sky.* London: Harrap, 1964.

Kee, Robert, and Joanna Smith. *We'll Meet Again.* London: Dent, 1984.

Keefan, John, ed. *Encyclopedia of World War II.* Maps, diagrams, charts. Essential for general survey.

Kelly, Terence. *Hurricane and Spitfire Pilots at War.* London: William Kimber, 1986.

Kemp, Sqn Ldr John. *Off to War with '054.* Braunton: Merlin, 1989. Author was a Battle of Britain pilot; account of a radar unit.

Kemp, P. K. *The Fleet Air Arm.* London: Herbert Jenkins, 1954.

Kendall, Alan. *Their Finest Hour.* London: Wayland, 1972.

Kennerley, Byron. *The Eagles Roar.* Washington: Zenger, 1941, 1981.

Kent, Gp Capt J. A. *One of the Few.* London: William Kimber, 1971.

Kent, Gp Capt John. "The Battle of Britain: Extracts from a Personal Diary." *The Polish Airman's Weekly Review* (1957).

Kent Aviation and Historical Research Society. *Flight in Kent.* Maidstone.

———. *Kent Airfields in the Battle of Britain.* Maidstone.

———. *Wings over Kent.* Maidstone.

Kidd, Janet Aitken. *The Beaverbook Girl: Growing Up in the 20s.* London: Collins, 1987. Daughter of the Minister for Aircraft Production.

Kimberley, Sgt Pilot Bob. *Home Sweet Home.* London: Webb and Bower/Michael Joseph.

King, Alison. *Golden Wings.* London: Arthur Pearson, 1956.

Kinsey, Gordon. *Martlesham Heath, 1917–73.* Lavenham, Suffolk: Terence Dalton, 1975.

———. *Orfordness, 1915–80.* Lavenham, Suffolk: Terence Dalton, 1983.

Knight, Dennis, and Gavin Lyall. "The Air War." Series in *Sunday Times Magazine,* 30 May–6 June 1965.

Knight, G. *Five Hundred Hours of the Blitz.* London: British Library.

Kosin, Rudiger. *The German Fighter since 1915.* London: Putnam, 1988.

Kostenuk/Griffin. *RCAF Squadrons.* Stevens, 1977.

Kuniczak, W. S. *Valedictory.* London: Michael Joseph, 1984. Fiction about a Polish squadron in the Battle.

Lanchberry, Edward. *Against the Sun.* London: Cassell, 1955. About Wg Cdr Roland Beamont. See also Beamont's *Phoenix into Ashes* and *My Part of the Sky.*

Lane, B. J. *Spitfire.* London: John Murray, 1942.

Leasor, James, and Kendal Burt. *The One That Got Away.* London: Collins, 1956.

Lecerf, J. L. "La Bataille Aerienne d'Angleterre." *Forces Aerienne Française,* 10 Année, no. 107.

Lee, Raymond E. *London Observer.* London: Hutchinson, 1972.

Leslie, Anita. *A Story Half Told.* London: Hutchinson, 1983.

Lewey, F. R. *Cockney Campaign.* London: Stanley Paul, 1947.
Lewin, Ronald. *Ultra Goes to War.* London: Hutchinson, 1978.
Lewis, C. D. *Word Over All: Airmen Broadcast.* London: Jonathan Cape, 1943.
Lewis, J. H. "London Diary." *Air Britain Digest* 4:5, 5:9 (1953).
Lewis, Peter. *A People's War.* London: Methuen, 1986.
Lillis, Steve, and Barry Hollis. *Military Airfields of the British Isles.* Omnibus ed. Irthlingborough: authors, 1987.
Liskutin, Sqn Ldr M. A. *Challenge in the Air.* London: William Kimber, 1988.
Lloyd, F. H. M. *Hurricane: The Story of a Great Fighter.* Harborough: Harborough Publishing, 1945.
Lomax, Judy. *Hanna Reitsch: Flying for the Fatherland.* London: John Murray, 1989. Female Luftwaffe pilot.
———. *Women of the Air.* London: John Murray, 1986.
Long, H. R., and H. R. P. Boorman. *Recalling the Battle of Britain.* Maidstone: Kent Messenger, 1965.
Longmate, Norman. *If Britain Had Fallen.* London: BBC/Hutchinson, 1974.
Lowe, Frank. *Twenty Years Ago They Broke the Luftwaffe.* Canada: Montreal Star, 1960.
Lucas, Laddie. *Flying Colours.* London: Hutchinson, 1981.
———, ed. *Out of the Blue.* London: Hutchinson, 1985.
Lynn, Vera. *Vocal Refrain.* London: W. H. Allen, 1975; Litton, Yorkshire: Magna Print Books, 1976. Autobiography of "The Forces Sweetheart," the most popular of the wartime vocalists.
———, with Robin Cross and Jenny de Gex. *We'll Meet Again.* London: Sidgwick and Jackson, 1989.
Macadam, John, and Gordon Anthony. *Air Aces.* London: Home and Van Thal, 1944.
McBride, Brenda. *Quiet Heroines.* London: Cakebreads, 1990.
Mack, Joanna, and Steve Humphries. *London at War.* London: Sidgwick and Jackson, 1985.
McKee, Alexander. *Strike from the Sky.* London: Souvenir Press, 1960; reprinted 1989.
Mackenzie, Wg Cdr K. W. *Hurricane Combat.* London: William Kimber, 1988.
MacKersey, Ian. *Into the Silk.* London: Robert Hale, 1956. Stories of the Caterpillar Club.
Macksey, Kenneth. *Invasion.* London: Arms and Armour Press, 1980. The fictitious invasion of England.
McLachlan, Ian. *Final Flights.* Personal investigations of over 100 crash sites.
Maclure, V. *Gladiators over Norway.* London, 1942.
Macmillan, Harold. *The Blast of War.* London: Harper and Row, 1967.
Macmillan, Capt N., MC AFC. *The RAF in the World War.* 2 vols. London: Harrap, 1942, 1944.
McRoberts, Douglas. *Lions Rampant.* London: William Kimber, 1985. 602 Squadron.
Magee, John Gillespie. "High Flight." In *More Poems from the Forces* (London, 1943).
———. *The Complete Works of John Magee.* Gloucester: This England, 1990.
Mahadie, Gp Capt Hamish. *Hamish: The Story of a Pathfinder.* London: Ian Allan, 1989.
Majdalany, Fred. *The Fall of Fortress Europe.* London: Hodder and Stoughton, 1969.
Marchant, Hilda. *Women and Children Last.* London: Golancz, 1941.
Margerison, Russell. *Boys at War.* 1943.
Marsh, L. G. *Polish Wings over Britain.* Max Love Publishing, 1943.

Martin, Gilbert. *Their Finest Hour.* London: Heinemann and Minerva, 1989. About Winston Churchill as prime minister.
Mason, Frank. *Battle over Britain.* London: McWhirter Twins, 1969.
———. *The Gloster Gladiator.* London: Macdonald, 1964.
———. *The Hawker Hurricane.* London: Macdonald, 1962; reprinted, Bourne End: Aston House, 1987.
Masters, David. *On the Wing.* London: Eyre and Spottiswoode.
———. *So Few.* London: Eyre and Spottiswoode, 1941.
Matthews, Very Rev. W. R. *St Paul's Cathedral in Wartime.* London: Hutchinson.
Mead, Peter. *The Eye in the Sky.* London: HMSO.
Mee, Arthur. *1940.* London: Hodder and Stoughton, 1941.
Middlebrook, Martin, and Chris Everitt. *Bomber Command War Diaries.* London and New York: Viking/Penguin, 1985. An operational reference book, 1939–45.
Middleton, Drew. *The Sky Suspended.* London: Secker and Warburg, 1960.
Milburn, Clara. *Mrs. Milburn's Diaries.* Ed. Peter Donnelly. London: Harrap, 1979.
Mitchell, A. W. *New Zealanders in the Air War.* London: Harrap, 1945.
Mitchell, Gordon. *R. J. Mitchell.* Olney: Nelson and Saunders. By the aircraft designer's son.
Moggeridge, Jackie. *Woman Pilot.* London: Michael Joseph, 1957.
Mole, Gp Capt Edward. *Happy Landings.* Wessex Aircraft.
Monday, David. *Complete Illustrated Encyclopedia of the World's Aircraft.* London.
Monks, Noel. *Squadrons Up!* London: Gollancz, 1940. About 1 and 73 Squadrons.
Moore, John. *The Fleet Air Arm.* London: Chapman and Hall, 1943.
Morgan, Eric, and Edward Shacklady. *Spitfire, the History.* Stanford: Key Publishing, 1987.
Moseley, Leonard. *The Battle of Britain.* London: Pan, 1969. The making of the film.
———, et al. *The Battle of Britain.* London: Time Life International Books, 1977.
———. *Faces from the Fire: Life of Sir Archibald McIndoe.* London: Weidenfeld and Nicolson, 1956. Burnt heroes saved by McIndoe.
Mouchotte, Rene. *The Mouchotte Diaries.* London: Staples Press, 1956.
Moulson, T. *The Flying Sword: 601 Squadron.* London: Macdonald, 1964.
Moyes, Patricia. *Johnny Underground.* London: Collins, 1965. Fiction.
Moyes, Philip J. R. *Bomber Squadrons of the Royal Air Force.* London: Macdonald and Jane's, 1976.
Munston, Ken, and John W. R. Taylor. *The Battle of Britain.* London: New English Library, 1976.
Murphy, Brendan. *Turncoat.* London: Macdonald, 1987.
Murray, Williamson. *Strategy for Defeat.* London: Collins, 1985.
Murrow, Edward R. *This Is London.* London: Cassell, 1941.
Nancarrow, F. G. *Gin y Daur, Glasgow's Fighter Squadron.* Glasgow: Collins, for the RAF Benevolent Fund, 1942.
———. *602 Squadron: Glasgow's Fighter Squadron.* Glasgow: Collins, 1942.
Narracott, A. H., ed. *In Praise of the Few.* London: Frederick Muller, 1947.
Neave, Airey. *Saturday at MI 9.* London: Hodder and Stoughton, 1969.
Neil, Wg Ddr Tom, DFC/bar AFC AE. *Gun Button to Fire.* London: William Kimber, 1987.
Nesbit, Roy Conyers. *Failed to Return.* Wellingborough: Patrick Stephens, 1989.
Norris, G. "McKellar, Scottish Ace." *RAF Flying Review*, London.

O'Brien, T. H. *Civil Defence.* London: Longmans, Green, 1955.

Offenberg, Jean. *Lonely Warrior.* London: Souvenir Press, 1956; Granada: Mayflower, 1969.

Ogden, Bob. *British Aviation Museums and Collections.* Stamford, Lincolnshire: Key Publishing, 1986. Updated regularly.

Ogley, Bob. *Biggin on the Bump.* Froglets Publications, 1990.

Orange, Vincent. *The Road to Biggin Hill.* Shrewsbury: Airlife, 1989. About Johnny Checketts.

———. *Sir Keith Park.* London: Methuen, 1984. For details see AIR DEFENCE OF GREAT BRITAIN.

Orde, Cuthbert. *Pilots of Fighter Command.* London. Drawings of a war artist.

Overy, R. J. *The Air War, 1939–45.* London: Europa Publications, 1980.

Oxspring, Gp Capt Bobby, DFC AFC. *Spitfire Command.* London: William Kimber, 1984.

Page, Geoffrey. *Tale of a Guinea Pig.* London: Pelham, 1981.

Park, K. R. "Background to the Blitz." *Hawker Siddeley Review* (December 1951).

Parkinson, Roger. *Dawn on Our Darkness.* London: Granada, 1977.

Parry, Simon. *Intruders over Britain.* New Malden: Air Research Publications, 1988. Luftwaffe night fighter offensive, 1940–45.

Passport to Exile. London: Hammersmith and Fulham Polish Community History, 1986.

Peden, Murray. *A Thousand Shall Fall.* Ottawa: Canadian Wings, 1979; Imperial War Museum, London.

Philpott, Bryan. *Eject! Eject!* London: Ian Allan, 1989. The story of ejection seats.

———. *Famous Fighter Aces.* London: Patrick Stephens.

———. *Fighters Defending the Reich.* Wellingborough: Patrick Stephens, 1989.

———. *German Bombers over England.* Wellingborough: Thorsons, 1989.

Pile, General Sir Frederick. *Ack Ack.* London: George Harrap.

Powers, Barry D. *British Air Defence, 1914–1939.* Texas, 1976.

Pretz, Bernard. *Dictionary of Military and Technical Abbreviations.* London: Routledge and Keegan Paul, 1983.

Price, Alfred. *The Hardest Day: 18 August 1940.* London: Macdonald and Jane's, 1979. Attacks on Kenley, Biggin Hill and on lll Squadron at Croydon.

———. *Spitfire at War.* London: Ian Allan, 1974, 1985.

———. In *Purnell's History of the Second World War*, Luftwaffe No. 10. London: Macdonald, 1989.

———. *Spitfire Story.* London: William Kimber, Arms and Armour, 1986.

Prins, Francis. Articles on film "Piece of Cake." *Fly Past* (October-November 1988).

———. "The One That Got Away." *Fly Past* (September 1990).

———. Two-part feature on the making of the film "The Battle of Britain," 1969. *Fly Past* (September 1989).

Probert, H., and S. Cox. *The Battle Re-thought: A Symposium on the Battle of Britain.* Shrewsbury: Airlife, 1991.

Pudney, John. *Ten Summers: Poems, 1933–43.* London: Bodley Head, 1944.

Purnell's History of the Second World War, no. 10. London: Macdonald, 1989.

Pushman, Muriel Gane. *We All Wore Blue.* London: Robson Books, 1989.

Quarrie, Bruce, ed. *Action Stations Vol. 10: Supplement and Index.* Wellingborough: Patrick Stephens and Thorsons, 1989.

Quill, Sir Jeffrey. *Spitfire: A Test Pilot's Story.* London: John Murray, 1983. Chief Test

Pilot for Supermarine, Jeffrey Quill's name is synonymous with Spitfire. Retired, he is President of The Spitfire Society.

———, with Sebastian Cox. *Birth of a Legend: The Spitfire.* London: Quiller Press, 1986.

RAF Flying Review 15, no. 2. Hitler's Battle of Britain Plan.

Ramsey, Winston G., ed. *The Battle of Britain, Then and Now.* London: After the Battle Publications, 1980.

Randal-Ford, J. M. *A Dorset Village's War Effort.* Bournemouth: Roman Press, 1945.

Rawlings, John D. *Fighter Squadrons of the RAF.* London: Macdonald and Jane's, 1976.

Rawnsley, C. F., and Robert Wright. *Night Fighter.* London: Collins, 1957. Prewar and night fighter training, with a foreword by John Cunningham.

Reid, John M. *The Battle of Britain: A short history* (commemorating the 20th Anniversary). London: Air Ministry, 1960.

———. *Some of the Few.* London: Macdonald, 1960. Collection of portraits by Cuthbert Orde.

Reid, P. R. *My Favourite Escape Stories.* London: Lutterworth Press, 1975.

Richards, Denis. *The Battle of Britain.* London: Purnell, 1966. In the series *History of the Second World War*, vol. 1, no. 12.

Richards, Denis, and Hilary St George Saunders. *Portal of Hungerford.* London: Heinemann, 1977.

———. *The Royal Air Force, 1939–45.* 3 vols. London: HMSO.

Richardson, Anthony. *Because of These.* London: Hodder and Stoughton, 1964.

———. *Wingless Victory: The Story of Sir Basil Embry's Escape.* London: Odhams, 1950.

Richey, Paul. *Fighter Pilot.* London: Batsford, 1942. First published anonymously, as was originally required by regulations.

Riley, Gordon. *British Aircraft Museums Directory.* Bourne End: Aston Publications, 1985.

———. *Vintage Aircraft Directory.* Bourne End: Aston Publications, 1985.

———, with Gordon Trant. *Spitfire Survivals Round the World.* Bourne End: Aston Publications, 1989.

Robertson, Bruce. *The Battle of Britain.* Sun Valley, CA: John W. Cales, Air Historians Model Books, 1976.

———. *Spitfire: The Story of a Famous Fighter.* London: Harleyford, 1960; London: Arms and Armour, 1962.

Robins, Gordon. *Fleet Street Blitz Diary.* London: Ernest Benn, 1944.

Robinson, Anthony, ed. *Air Power, the World's Air Forces.* London: Orbis Books, 1980. Foreword by Air Vice Marshal Stewart Menaul.

Robinson, Derek. *Piece of Cake.* London: Hamish Hamilton, 1983; New York: Alfred A. Knopf, 1984. See also television film for UK, 1986; article by Francois Prins in *Fly Past* (October/November 1988).

Rolls, Flt Lt W. T., DFC DFM. *Spitfire Attack.* London: William Kimber, 1987. Good outline of pilot initial training. Lists all pilots of 72 Sqn in Battle of Britain with "score sheet," records and a good index.

Rothenstein, Sir William. *Men of the RAF.* Oxford: Oxford University Press, 1942. Portrait drawings.

Rouse, Wally. *Born Again: Spitfire PR 19.* London.

Rudd, Anthony. *One Boy's War.* London: Quartet, 1990.

Rudel, Hans Ulrich. *Stuka Pilot.* London: Euphoria Books and Macdonald.
Sanders, James. *The Time of My Life.* Auckland, N.Z.: Minerva, 1967.
———. *Venturer Courageous.* Auckland, N.Z.: Hutchinson, 1983.
Sands, Fg Off R. P. D. *Treble One—lll Squadron.* Privately printed.
Saunders, Hillary St George, et al. *The Battle of Britain.* London: Alan Wingate, 1969. An official account of the Battle was first published by the Ministry of Information, London, in 1941. The author's name was not given but later disclosed by Tandem's (London, 1969) to be Saunders. Saunders had compiled the account from official sources and included Richard Hillary's *The Last Enemy* (London: Macmillan, 1942), and Cajus Bekker's *The Luftwaffe War Diaries* (London: Macdonald, 1967; Gerhard Stalling Verlag, 1964).
Saward, Gp Capt Dudley. *Bomber Harris: The Authorised Biography of Sir Arthur Harris.* London: Cassell, 1984.
———. *The Bomber's Eye.* London: Cassell, 1959.
———. *Victory Denied.* London: Cassell. The rise of air power and the defeat of Germany, 1920–45.
Settle. Mary Lee. *All the Brave Promises.* London: Heinemann, 1966; Pandora, 1984. The WAAFs.
Shapland, Jean. *The Memories Linger On.* St Eval, Cornwall: privately printed, 1989.
Sharp, Martin C. *Flight: The Quizzer Book.* London: Owlet Books, 1975. Juvenile.
Shaw, Michael. *Twice Vertical—1 Squadron.* London: Macdonald, 1971.
Shennan, Noel. *Combat Aircraft of the Battle of Britain.* Dandenong, Australia: Kookaburra Technical Publications, 1976.
Shiver, William L. *The Rise and Fall of the Third Reich.* London: Pan Books, 1964. To be read in conjunction with books on the Luftwaffe.
Shores, Christopher, and Clive Williams. *Aces High.* London: Neville Spearman, 1986.
———. *Battle of Britain: Hurricane, Spitfire and Messerschmitt.* London: Osprey, 1969.
Simpson, William, DFC. *One of Our Pilots Is Safe.* London: Hamish Hamilton, 1942.
Sims, E. *Fighter Pilots.* London: Cassell, 1967.
Skinner, Michael. *Red Flag: Training For Fighter Pilots.* London: William Kimber.
Slee, Daphne. *That Great Hunter.* London: Peter Davies, 1951. Fiction.
———. *The Poor Wise Man.* London: Peter Davies, 1952. Fiction.
Slessor, Sir John. *The Central Blue.* London: Cassell, 1956.
Smith, D. J. *Britain's Military Airfields, 1939–45.* Wellingborough: Patrick Stephens, 1989.
———. *High Ground Relics.* Wellingborough: Patrick Stephens.
———. *The Military Airfields of the North East and Northern Ireland,* vol. 7, Action Station Series. Wellingborough: Patrick Stephens, 1989.
———. *The Military Airfields of Wales and the North West,* vol. 3, Action Stations series. Wellingborough: Patrick Stephens and Thorsons, 1981.
Smith, N. D. *The Battle of Britain.* London: Faber and Faber, 1962. Men and Events series. Twelve months from May 1940-1941.
Smith, Ted. *Spitfire Diary.* London: William Kimber, 1988.
South African Air Force. On microfilm, PRO AIR 54.
Spaight, J. M. *The Battle of Britain, 1940.* London: Geoffrey Bles, 1941.
Spiller, H. J. *Ticket to Freedom.* London: William Kimber.
Stahl, Peter. *The Diving Eagle.* London: William Kimber.

Stanford, Derek. *Inside the '40s: literary memories 1937-57.* London: Sidgwick and Jackson, 1977. Background only, has a few RAF references.

Stanhope, Palmer Robert. *No Battle of Britain (Tank Trap 1940).* Ilfracombe: Stockwell, 1976.

Steinhilper, Ulrich. *Spitfire on My Tail: The Battle from the Other Side.* Keston, Kent: Independent Books, 1989.

Stevenson, Sqn Ldr Derek Leyland, DFC. *Five Crashes Later: The Story of a Fighter Pilot.* London: William Kimber, 1988.

Stevenson, Sir William. *A Man Called Intrepid: The Secret War, 1939–45.* London: Macmillan, 1976; London: Sphere, 1977. About the British Security Coordination Intelligence Service in New York.

Stewart, Adrian. *Hurricane.* London: William Kimber, 1982.

Stockman, Flt Lt Rocky. *The History of RAF Manston.* Kent: RAF Manston, 1986.

Stokes, Doug. *Fighting in the Air.* London: William Kimber.

———. *Paddy Finucane, Fighter Ace.* London: William Kimber, 1983. Biography.

———. *Wings Aflame.* London: William Kimber, 1984.

Storrer, J. D. *Behind the Scenes in an Aircraft Factory.* London: Phoenix House, 1965.

Sturtivant, Ray. *The Anson File.* Tonbridge: Air Britain, 1988.

———. *Fleet Air Arm at War.* London: Ian Allan, 1982.

———. *Squadrons of the Fleet Air Arm.* Tonbridge: Air Britain, 1984. By squadron number, date, place and equipment. On open shelves at the PRO.

Sutton, Gp Capt Barry. *The Way of a Pilot.* London: Macmillan, 1942.

Sutton, Sqn Ldr H. T. *Raiders Approach.* Aldershot: Gale and Polden, 1953.

Swanborough, Gordon. *United States Military Aircraft.* London: Putnam, 1963, 1989.

Sweetman, Bill. *Spitfire.* London: Jane's, 1980. Beautifully detailed drawings and diagrams by Rikyn Watanabe.

Tamplin, J. M. A., and P. E. Abbott. *British Gallantry Awards.* Enfield, London: Guinness Superlatives, 1971.

Taylor, Eric. *Women Who Went to War, 1938–46.* London: Grafton, 1989.

Taylor, John W. R. *The Royal Air Force.* Oxford: Oxford University Press, 1965.

Taylor, John W. R., and K. G. Munson. *The Battle of Britain.* London: New English Library, 1976.

Taylor, Telford. *The Breaking Wave: The German Defeat in the Summer of 1940.* London: Weidenfeld & Nicolson, 1967.

Taylor, Robert. *The Air Combat Paintings of Robert Taylor.* Newton Abbot: David and Charles, 1987.

Teague, Dennis C. *Roborough, Plymouth City Airport 1929-89.* Plymouth, 1990.

Templewood, 1st Viscount Samuel, *Empire of the Air.* London: Collins, 1957.

———. *The Unbroken Thread.* London, 1949. Author was in the RAF.

Terraine, John. *The Right of the Line.* London: Hodder and Stoughton, 1985.

Terry, Roy. *Women in Khaki.* London: Columbus, 1988.

Thomas, G. *Shoulder the Sky.* London: A. Barker, 1959.

Thompson, H. L. *New Zealanders with the RAF.* 3 vols. Wellington: Dept. of National Affairs, 1959.

Thompson, J. B. *Charter Hall.* New Malden, 1989.

Thompson, Lawrence. *1940: Year of Legend, Year of History.* London: Collins, 1966.

Tidy, Douglas. *I Fear No Man.* London: Macdonald, 1972. 74 Squadron.

Tilbury, Ann. *The Battle of Britain.* London: Macdonald, 1981; London, New York:

Simon and Schuster, 1988. With illustrations by Michael Turner, President of Guild of Aviation Artists. For children.

Tolliver, R. *The Blond Knight of Germany.* London: Barker, 1970.

Townsend, Peter. *Duel in the Dark.* London: Harrap, 1986. Sequel to *Duel of Eagles.*

———. *Duel of Eagles.* London: Weidenfeld and Nicholson, 1970.

———. "La Bataille d'Angleterre." *Forces Aerienne Française,* No. 61–65 (August/September 1955); *Paris Match,* 17 September and 24 September 1966.

———. *Time and Chance.* London: Collins, 1978.

Trevor, Elleston. *Squadron Airborne.* London: Willim Heinemann, 1951. Fiction.

Trevor-Roper, H. R., ed. *Hitler's War Directives, 1939-45.* London, 1964.

Turner, Barry. *The Writer's Handbook.* London: Macmillan, 1988. For addresses of suitable magasines and publishers which may have other material.

Turner, John Frayn. *The Bader Tapes.* London: Midas Books. The Bader Wing.

———. *British Aircraft of World War II.* London: Sidgwick and Jackson, 1975.

Vader, John. *Spitfire.* London: Pan Books, 1972.

Victor, John A. *Time Out: American Airmen in Stalag Luft I.* London: Arms and Armour Press.

Wakefield. Kenneth. *Luftwaffe Encore: September 1940.* London: William Kimber, 1979.

Walker, Charles. "The Forgotten Ace." *A Legacy of Scots: Scottish Achievments.* Edinburgh: Mainstream, 1989. Chapter on Archie McKeller DSO DFC/bar, who was killed eight hrs after the Battle had officially ended, so name not on the Roll.

Walker, O. *Sailor Malan.* London: Cassell, 1953.

Wallace, G. *Biggin Hill.* London: Putnam, 1957.

Waller, Jane, and Michael Vaughan-Rees. *Women in Uniform.* London: Macmillan, 1989.

Wallington. Neil. *Fireman*! London: David and Charles, 1979.

———. *Fireman at War.* London: David and Charles, 1981.

Ward, Arthur. *A Nation Alone: Battle of Britain, 1940.* London: Osprey and the RAF Museum, 1989.

Ward, Wg Cdr, ed. *Spitfire and Hurricane Tribute.* London: Ian Allan, 1986. Battle of Britain Memorial Flight 1986.

Ward-Jackson, C. H., ed. *Airman's Song Book.* Sylvan Press, n.d.

———. *It's a Piece of Cake.* Sylvan Press, n.d.

———. *RAF Short Stories.* N.d.

Watkins, David. *Fear Nothing: History of 501 Squadron Royal Auxiliary Air Force.* Edenbridge: Newton, 1990.

Waugh, Evelyn. *Put Out More Flags.* London. Fiction.

Weale, John A., and Richard F. Barker. *Combat Aircraft of World War II.* London: Bracken Books, 1985.

Webb, Arthur. *Battle over Kent.* Chilham: Kent Battle of Britain Museum, 1977.

Weir. F/O A. N. C. *Verses of a Fighter Pilot.* London: Faber and Faber, 1937.

Wentzel, Fritz. *Single or Return?* London: William Kimber. Story of von Werra.

West, Nigel. *M16: British Secret Intelligence Service Operations, 1909–45.* London: Weidenfeld and Nicolson, 1983.

———. *A Matter of Trust, MI 5, 1954–70, London.* London: Weidenfeld and Nicolson, 1982.

———, and Richard Deacon. *Spy.* London: BBC, 1980.

Whiting, Charles. *Britain Under Fire.* London: Century, 1985.

Williams, Peter, Ted Harrison. *McIndoe's Army.* London: Pelham, 1979. The story of the gifted surgeon who pioneered skin graft surgery on burned aircrew at his hospital in East Grinstead. Has full list of books by and members of the Guinea Pig Club. Book was used as documentary made by Thames Television.

Williamson, Gordon. *Aces of the Reich.* London: Cassell, 1989.

Willis, John. *Churchill's Few.* London: Michael Joseph, 1985. No bibliography but good photos and interviews.

Willis, Steve, and Barry Hollis. *Military Airfields of the British Isles.* Kettering, 1988. Available from authors.

Wilson. Eunice. "An American in the RAF." *Nostalgia* (October 1989).

———. *Records of the RAF: How to Find the Few.* Birmingham: Federation of Family History Societies, 1991.

Winchester, Barry. *Eighty Four Days—The Battle of Britain Remembered.* London: Selma, 1974.

Winslade, Richard. *The Battle of Britain Memorial Flight.* London: Osprey.

Winter, D. *The First of the Few.* London: Allen Lane, 1982.

Winterbotham, F. W. *Secret and Personal.* London, 1969.

———. *The Ultra Secret.* London: Weidenfeld and Nicholson, 1969.

Wood, D., and D. Dempster. *The Narrow Margin.* London: Arrow Books, 1969; London: Hutchinson, 1961. Day by day account, with statistics and movements.

Wright, Robert. *Dowding and the Battle of Britain.* London: Macdonald, 1969. Biography of the Air Officer Commanding Fighter Command, the architect of the Battle without whom it could not have been fought, let alone won.

Writers and Artists' Year Book. Annual. For newspaper and publishers' addresses in UK. *Writers' Market.* As above in USA.

Wykeham, Peter. *Fighter Command.* London: Putnam, 1960.

Wynn, Humphrey. *Angels 22.* London: Arrow Books, 1977. About George Barclay.

———. *Royal Air Force Quarterly* (September 1974). Article commemorating the Battle of Britain and about George Barclay. Dr Wynn is an Air Historical Branch historian.

Wynne, Kenneth. *A Clasp for the Few.* Auckland, N.Z.: privately printed, 1981. New Zealanders in the Battle of Britain.

———. *Fighter Pilot.* London: William Kimber, 1976.

Wynne, Kenneth G. *Men of the Battle of Britain.* Norwich: Gliddon Books, 1989. Biographical studies of everyone in the Battle of Britain Association, then and now; a Who was Who of pilots and aircrew.

Young, Gordon. *In Trust and Treason.* London: Studio Vista, 1959.

Ziegler, Frank H. *The Story of 609 Squadron: Under the White Rose.* London: Macdonald, 1971.

Zuckerman, Solly. *From Apes to Warlords.* London: Hamish Hamilton, 1978. Adviser to the Minister of Aircraft Production.

FINAL NOTE

And still the grateful tributes continue. On Remembrance Sunday, commemorated at the Cenotaph in Whitehall, London, on the nearest Sunday to the 11th November, the date on which the Armistice was signed in 1918, the traditional two minutes silence is observed at 11 o'clock and at War Memorials all over the country.

On Battle of Britain Day, 15 September, every year since 1940, we remember THE FEW who saved us from defeat and destruction in the skies above us as we watched in that fateful summer.

Biggin Hill July 1947

On Weald of Kent I watched once more
Again I heard the grumbling roar
Of fighter planes; yet none were near
And all around the sky was clear
Borne on the wind a whisper came
'Though men grow old, they stay the same'
And then I knew, unseen to eye
The ageless Few were sweeping by.

—Lord Balfour of Inchyre

Per Ardua Ad Astra
(Through Endeavour to the Stars)
—motto of the Royal Air Force

Index

About the Author

EUNICE WILSON is a professional writer and freelance accredited researcher at the Public Record office, London. Among her earlier works are numerous articles in *RAF News*, *Fly Past*, and *Airmail*, as well as a guide to the RAF, *How to Find the Few*, *RAF Quiz Book*, and the *D-Day Quiz Book*.

www.ingramcontent.com/pod-product-compliance
Lightning Source LLC
Chambersburg PA
CBHW070442100426
42812CB00004B/1183
9780313282164